TREMBLING
FAITH

TAYLOR TURKINGTON

TREMBLING FAITH

How a Distressed
Prophet Helps Us
Trust God in a
Chaotic World

PUBLISHING
BRENTWOOD, TENNESSEE

Published by B&H Publishing Group
Brentwood, Tennessee

Dewey Decimal Classification: 234.2
Subject Heading: FAITH / BIBLE. O.T. HABAKKUK / PRAYER

Cover design and collage by Ligia Teodosiu.
Cover collage images by © Paulpaladin/Dreamstime.
com; © Allagreeg/Dreamstime.com; © nemalo/123rf.com;
Piyaset/Shutterstock; Everett Collection/Shutterstock;
Anastasiia Smiian/Shutterstock. Author photo by Natalie
Kristeen Photography.

1 2 3 4 5 6 · 26 25 24 23

For my daughter RAT:
May you live by faith in our just God,
even if you tremble, my darling.

And

For our brothers and sisters
around the world who face
injustices we can only imagine:
May His justice and faithfulness
be your joy today.

Acknowledgments

This book wouldn't exist without prodding and encouragement from a handful of wise women, many of whom have sat with me and counseled me as we talked about teaching the Bible in public settings and in books. Thank you, friends, for pushing me to write and reminding me that the Lord would help.

I'm immensely indebted to friends who read portions of this book to make it better: Todd Miles, Rachel Gilson, Blair Linne, Hannah Nation, Shar Walker, Matt Mikalatos, and Amy McCormick. And the pastors and leaders at my church who dove into it to offer feedback: Jose Zayas, Ryan Doucet, Margaret Rhoades, Steve Marshman, Tracy Nordyke, and Jodi Hughes.

I wouldn't have finished a dissertation on Habakkuk if it wasn't for Dr. Steve Mathewson who supervised me and made me finish. Thank you, Steve.

To the friends who listened to my processing, even when I was discouraged, in pain, or sleep deprived, and prayed me over the finish line—what a gift you are. As are my parents and mother-in-law who supported us and distracted a three-year-old who wanted desperately to write the book.

Don, thank you for this journey together and your support as my agent. I am grateful! Ashley, you have made this work better in your advising and editing, and it has been a joy to partner with you, friend.

To Matt who has loved me and heard more ramblings on faith in an unjust world than anyone—you alone know how much you have made this possible. I'm so glad I get to do life with you; I love you to the end of our days.

To the God who gives life to his people of faith—your Word is our ground, and your welcome is our hope. Your just and loving character fuels our endurance. We live because of you.

You are worthy of all our praise.

Contents

Introduction

Faith in the Midst of Chaos

Trembling, I climbed the five-hundred-year-old stone stairs leading to the ridge above. My mind raced. *Why God? How is it okay for her to go through this? She should have never had to deal with such fear and lies.* The steps went on, seemingly endless and obviously uneven. The old stairway crossed the roads that switchbacked up to the cliff that stood towering over the city where I lived. As I walked, my emotions swirled, and I prayed. The world around me felt out of control.

When have you been hit sideways with the pain, unfairness, or wrongdoing around you? Fear, confusion, or outrage churn, perhaps all coming to the surface within the same hour. So it was as I shuffled up the hillside in Rijeka,[1] Croatia.

Months after finishing university, I had moved with a ministry team to Croatia in Eastern Europe. Beautiful Rijeka was home for two years. The city sits on the

---

1. Sounds like "ree-YEH-kuh"

stunning Adriatic Sea in the northwest corner of the country, just opposite the top of the Italian "boot."

Though, after just a few weeks in the city, the brokenness of the world felt painfully accentuated. The impact of the historical conflict became apparent. Like an explosion that ricocheted through the community, the Balkan wars had left their mark on unnumbered lives. Trudging up the stairway, the misuse of power on a much more minor scale was at the forefront of my mind as certain authorities intimidated and manipulated as they wanted. On the most personal stage, suffering and heartbreak seemed to follow those I loved, instead of the goodness and mercy for which I was praying.

God, she should never have had to deal with religious leaders who use power for their own gain. It should never be that she would fear violence when offered to learn more about you. My prayers tumbled out as I slowed my ascent, feeling each of the hundreds of steps. *And he shouldn't be losing his apartment because of the greed of the authorities.* Then my thoughts turned to the ethnic minority community I had visited living in the hills surrounding the dump. *How can prejudice happen like this? Lord, what are you doing?*

I walked up the Trsat[2] stairway, step after step, thinking of the pilgrims who walk it on their knees. While I wasn't going to join them, I felt their desperation. Shaking a bit from being out of breath, I paused

---

2. Pronounced "ter-SAT," where the "sat" rhymes with "taught"

and turned to look where I'd come. I could see the Mrtvi[3] Kanal running through the center of town, shining in the distance. It literally means "Dead Canal." The brackish water smelled dead when you were near, reminding you of the unseemly contents that were likely in it. One of the war monuments sat over it on a bridge, declaring the stand courageous Croatians took and betraying the deep wounds the region had from violent conflict.

Friend, there's a world out of control—abuse of power, injustice, suffering. It was hitting me between the eyes. Have you been there? Spewing fiery words to an invisible conversation partner about the brokenness of the world?

As I kept walking, I passed by the old neighborhoods built into the hillside, and after more than five hundred steps, I arrived at the Catholic church dedicated to Mary, Church of the Lady of Trsat. The beauty designed to move me to worship didn't stir me that day, and I kept walking.

I turned down a side street, and finally at my destination, I walked into the ancient castle of Trsat. It looked strange nestled in the middle of an industrial city with concrete buildings lining the streets. Yet there it was, its ancient construction supporting a view of the city in all its glory. This was why I'd come.

The ancient nature of the castle felt like solid ground beneath my feet, for it reminded me that faithful believers had prayed desperate prayers in this land for

---

3. Pronounced "MERT-vy"

thousands of years. Coupled with the view, somehow you would feel grounded and gliding simultaneously. From the edge of the castle, one could see the industrial port, the sprawling houses with their terra-cotta roofs, and the canal flowing through, sparkling in the sun. It no longer looked dead at this elevation. The boardwalk with its shops gleamed, and the island off the coast would magically remind you of the many more you could not see. And the water—the dazzling blues summoned to mind why people love the Mediterranean Sea. It was hard not to feel your breathing slow as you took in the seascape.

Seeing the entire city, as a taste of how God sees, was why I came there to pray. The soaring panorama loosened my tongue to honesty, and the words flowed. *Broken, God. How long will you leave this world broken?* I returned to pray at that castle many times over the years I lived there. Trembling with weakness. With outrage. With overwhelmed sobs, or desperate weariness. The view from the medieval fortress gave me something—unleashing my frank pleas to God and bolstering me with a view to see the city with faith. Standing at the heights, it's as if I could see above the injustice. I could arrive trembling in weakness and leave trembling in awe.

Trembling at Home

While it may feel foreign to trek up a cliff in Europe, weighty with prayers about oppression, the injustices surround us no matter where we live. I stood recently on Mount Tabor, a hill in my city of Portland, Oregon, and looked out over the city to protest-pray about people stuck in suffering.

How long is it going to be like this? God, what are you doing? It's like we're in this pit, without any help, and you've put us here. I prayed, mimicking the sons of Korah;[4] I bet you've prayed like that.

Perhaps there's no lookout near your place where you pray fiery petitions, but let me tell you that a biblical prophet has a view for us. This prophet is going to take us on a journey. He will march us up the stairs to a height. We may complain about the injustices alongside him; we may be weary from the weight of the wrongdoing around us. We might question God's faithfulness or yell about what we've seen, but the journey of this prophet is what we need.

He models for us the way faithful believers have prayed for thousands of years and has a lens through which we can look at the chaos of this world and still have faith, even if we tremble.

His message doesn't only offer more facts about God and his character. It's not that we have more biblical literacy by reading this book of the Bible (though you will), it's that, by its message, we can now see. The light shines on the landscape of this chaotic world, and we can have the view to understand and hope.

4. The sons of Korah wrote multiple psalms, including Psalm 88:4–7, which resembles my prayer.

How Long, Lord?

If I drew you my life's time line, there would be red dots periodically where things got hard, and I could label them "when I ended up in Habakkuk." In high school, I read it to deal with questions of inequity and mistreatment others faced. (Though I'll tell you, I skipped some of the confusing parts.) A few years later, I read it as my health took a turn for the worse, and the length of my life was uncertain. In my first years working out of college, living in Croatia, I read it when I was exasperated, feeling like God wasn't answering any of my desperate prayers. I studied it when I sat in a hospital room hearing about experimental surgery options. I read it when I faced discrimination and outrage in my own heart. I wrote my doctoral dissertation on it when my family went through one of the most excruciating seasons because of choices others made. I kept coming back to the three-chaptered book toward the end of the Old Testament.

Why? Habakkuk models how to speak to God when life is agonizing. He teaches us a way to face the corruption around us without sticking our heads in the sand, becoming so angry we explode, or so depressed we wither. It's a way of faith. Faith like that which made Abram upright before God even when he couldn't see how the promises would be realized. Faith that brings perseverance. Faith that leads to real, full life. Faith that isn't cliché, but resilient and gritty. Faith that sees what God is doing on the horizon and today.

Habakkuk may be the last place you would think to look. The short prophetic books in the middle of our Bibles often are the ones still tinted gold on the edges— they haven't gotten the same amount of read time. It's understandable. The Minor Prophets proclaim strong poetic messages that sound abstract, harsh, and sometimes just plain complicated.

But trust me. When suffering beats us up and we feel like the bad guys are winning, the journey of Habakkuk shows us the way. It shows us that God sees exactly what is broken, and he is working. When our minds are filled with doubts, anger, and confusion, the words of Habakkuk meet us with God's plan. You see, Habakkuk speaks of trembling faith that faces the chaos and lives.

The Lord truly welcomes our cries, our protests, and our wrestling. I pray you would know as you read that he is the God who gives life and does justice. And he has a lifeline of a message for you from an ancient prophet who wants to help you see.

Section 1

LAMENT AND HOPE

Chapter 1

Faith and Paying Attention

"God, please help."

*How long, Lᴏʀᴅ, must I call for help and you do not listen
or cry out to you about violence and you do not save?*

(Hab. 1:2)

Jill[1] didn't talk much when he was present, which was usually the case at church. Questions addressed to her made her eyes go wide. Time awkwardly ticked by, and then she would shift to look at him. He would answer, a well-composed man who knew how to read a room. When her husband wasn't around, Jill was chatty. She made jokes and talked about what she was learning from the Lord. In her work life, Jill managed a successful professional career, and her eyes lit up when she talked about her kids.

Something seemed . . . off.

---

1. Her name has been changed for privacy.

11

In the quiet of a meeting designated for other purposes, Jill stared at the ground while she described her husband's words, voice, and his anger. His "episodes." She said she was "just asking for prayer." She needed patience and to do what honored Jesus as she interacted with him, she explained. Details of his controlling behavior and her and her children's fear tumbled out in bits and pieces. If you were in the room, you would have guessed, as I did, that there was more to the story. She was so hesitant—you'd wonder if this was just scratching the surface of the emotional and physical pain. And it was.

Maybe you're like me, and you haven't had similar conversations just once but several times. If we are paying attention, we will see a lot of "off" around us. You may have never heard the timid appeals for help in an abusive marriage, but I bet you have noticed things that appeared unjust. Cracks in the façade that showed injustice is real. People hurt. Bullies winning. The right action left undone or the wrong action bringing harm. When we pay attention, we have to acknowledge this world is gut-wrenchingly broken.

Many of us will read a description of mistreatment and nod along from experience, memories bringing a fire to our chest. Others hear words about injustice, and it all feels distant. The deep desire to downplay evil stirs, perhaps even subconsciously.

Reading Habakkuk beckons us to acknowledge a foundational principle God reveals through Old Testament prophets—*you have to see the evil*. We must look around at what is happening in the world and see it for what it is.

It's our own selfish actions and apathy toward others. It's the trauma done to children in some families. It's the bullies in powerful places. It's genocidal wars. No matter where you find it—whether it's external, out there in the world, or internal, wreaking havoc in your own heart—you cannot pretend wickedness doesn't exist. As Habakkuk helps us see, *we can't carry on like it doesn't.*

If you were hesitant to dig into the book of Habakkuk before, this statement about facing the horror of the world may have added fuel to your exit plan. Don't give up! While Habakkuk will push us to deal with the chaos around us, he is going to tell us the truth we need to know.

The Prophets and Paying Attention

One thing is for sure, God's spokespeople writing in the Bible will tell it to us straight—we must pay attention.

As one scholar puts it: "The situation of a person immersed in the prophet's words is one of being exposed to a ceaseless shattering of indifference, and one needs a skull of stone to remain callous to such blows."[2] The Bible paints the prophets as those who jolt

---

2. Abraham J. Heschel, *The Prophets*, 1st Perennial Classics ed. (New York: Harper Perennial Modern Classics, 2001), xxv.

us awake and force us to see what is happening and what God says about such things.

They are the watchmen signaling with waving arms, often to people wanting to look away. Look up and see the evil done against others (Micah 2:1–2), the prophets said. See the impact of your own choices on the vulnerable (Isa. 10:1–2). See the disobedience of God's people (Zeph. 3:4). *God sees the ways we've gotten things super wrong, guys, and he's coming to do something about it. Get ready. We might not be paying attention, but he is.*

A real estate agent I once rented from held a similar attitude as God's people. She wanted to smooth over any problems rather than look closer at the grave state of things. Walking up to the apartment I would rent, the agent pointed up, saying, "Look how lovely the balcony is!"

As we got inside the flat, her tone changed about the platform hanging off the fourth story residence. "Oh, don't look at it closely. Walk right past those terrace doors, and do not go out there now." If you ignored her advice and chose to examine it, you would realize the concrete porch had cracks running through it, particularly where it was precariously attached. It leaned away from the building, sloping down, as if beginning the dive it would one day take. Stepping onto the balcony would have been taking our lives in our hands, along with the stream of people walking on the street below. The real estate agent preferred to smile, ignore the cracks, and continue on.

Similarly, it would be easy for some of us—and beneficial at times—to look away from the wrong done around us. We much prefer the aesthetics that way. Yet there are consequences to indifference, just like there would have been if we held lunch on that balcony. We should not be surprised by discipline from the Lord if we choose not to pay attention to the discrepancy between our community's actions and God's righteous standard, just as the prophets warned in Israel. The Lord told them it was because they did not listen; it was because they didn't pay attention to his words that they were sent into exile (Jer. 29:18–19).[3]

Alright, you may think, *suppose we pay attention to the injustice and brokenness around us, even when we want to look away. Then what? Do we acknowledge it then put on a happy face? What do we do with anger, sadness, and powerlessness in the face of the horrific evil of this world that we cannot stop?*

This is exactly where we join Habakkuk on his journey. You see, this prophet's book isn't a collection of his messages from God like some other prophetic books. Nor is it a narrative of his life, like the book of Jonah.

Habakkuk does something different—he invites us into his conversation with God, like we're sitting in on his prayer meeting. We have a front-row seat to Habakkuk's

---

3. Though the Hebrew word here is *shema*, meaning "to listen," it is translated "pay attention" in the ESV. The verb more often translated as "pay attention" (*keshav*) is used to describe their failure to obey and the reason for their coming punishment in Zechariah 1:4 and 7:11.

wrestling, listening, bravery, and gritty faith. *We get to see what real faith in the middle of chaos, wrongdoing, and suffering actually looks like.*

But before we jump in further, let's set the scene a bit.

Habakkuk's Chaos

Habakkuk's situation can feel far from our lived experience, but it really isn't. He lived in a time of political chaos, violence, and a whole lot of wrong. He had witnessed strong leadership, and even revival. Then, he saw it all crumble before his eyes as leaders lived for their own power and believed in their own authority. Oppression, danger, and hardship enveloped his society. Sound familiar?

Pharoah Neco of Egypt decided to dabble in the politics of Judah by doing two things. First, after he'd killed Judah's good King Josiah, he exiled Josiah's son who had begun to rule. Second, Pharoah put another of Josiah's sons in charge—with strings attached, of course. (He had already killed one king and ousted the next; his dominance was established.) Pharoah even changed the new king's name from Eliakim ("God will establish") to Jehoiakim ("the LORD will establish"), inserting God's covenant name the Lord Yahweh instead of the more generic "God." Was this supposed to assure the Jewish people of his leadership? Was Pharaoh claiming divine right to rule over God's people? As if the name of the

Lord would bring any comfort when it was in the mouth of a cruel foreign ruler.

Our friend, Habakkuk, lived under the rule of King Jehoiakim. It wasn't a virtuous reign.

Do we see leaders around us live for their own power so that injustice seeps in? Have we seen the choice of self-protection and self-benefit instead of caring for those in need and those in the right? Time and again. In organizations, in nations, and sadly, at times, in churches.

As I write this, the global Christian community is still reeling from the news of a major Christian leader who was found to be a systematic sexual abuser. Some dear to me are mourning the broken systems of foster care and the impact on children. And I bet you've seen some situation or issue unravel in recent years that made your stomach turn. Maybe it's human trafficking. Or racism. Or the needs of children. Or unfair treatment of some vulnerable population. Here's what I want you to know in all of that: Habakkuk gets it. He was facing what we still see in our world: injustice.

King Jehoiakim, the token king for Egypt, encouraged anything but righteous faith in the Lord of his name. "Change your worship to what aligns you with the right people," would have been his sermon title (Jer. 25:1–6; Ezek. 8:5–17). Additional idolatry brought gain in his mind. Thus, he seemed to ignore the feasts and temple-worship that God required of his people, only using religion for what served him.

Again, does this sound familiar? Leaders who would use religion to manipulate others and gain allegiance and power, all under the banner of God's name? A quick scroll through various types of media will prove that our present reality is littered with such stories.

Adding to his horrific reign, Jehoiakim raised taxes to fuel his own lifestyle and to pay Egypt their tribute. His lavish buildings required slave labor and abuse of his own people. The people lived in poverty as he built his costly homes. He clashed with Jeremiah, whom God used to warn him of coming judgment (Jer. 22, 25).

What was Jehoiakim's response to God's correction? He burned Jeremiah's scroll bit by bit, literally silencing the Word of God written for the people. To further silence the prophets who would dare to speak against him, Jehoiakim sent out assassins. Habakkuk faced the threat of death! The result of the abandonment of God's justice in Judah's society was chaos.[4] The silencing of correcting voices wasn't unique in Habakkuk's time.

Leadership punishing those who want to serve the Lord describes the circumstances for many across the world today. While our government may not have been taken over by a Pharoah, the misuse of power is around us, injustice and corruption too, even in the name of the Lord.

---

4. Elizabeth Achtemeier, *Nahum–Malachi: Interpretation: A Bible Commentary for Teaching and Preaching* (Atlanta: Westminster John Knox Press, 1988), 35.

Though we'd rather look away sometimes, faith requires us to pay attention.

Habakkuk's Paying Attention

In the midst of all that Habakkuk saw, he spoke. Habakkuk had a burden weighing on him after paying attention, and he told God about it.[5] It's as if the prophet puts his arm around us and invites us into his prayer.

> **How long, LORD, must I call for help**
> **and you do not listen**
> **or cry out to you about violence**
> **and you do not save?**
> **(Hab. 1:2)**

Habakkuk used God's divine name, revealed to Moses: Yahweh ("LORD"). It reminds us that this is no ordinary master, but the Lord who is in relationship with his people, and this clearly isn't the first time Habakkuk brought up the chaos and pain around him. He'd stood there waving his arms in frustration before, like I did on Mount Tabor. Through poetry and repetition, Habakkuk told God what has been happening—he'd been calling out for help, and God wasn't helping.

Habakkuk may appear brash to us as he accuses God of dallying instead of saving. But Habakkuk's prayer

---

5. The word *oracle* used in some translations of Habakkuk 1:1 (ESV) can also be translated as "burden." This is usually a term used to describe prophetic messages to foreign nations and can imply a weight or load carried with the message.

wasn't impertinent; it was like a child, scared and hurting, asking for help from a devoted parent. An intimate
dialogue with a trusted God. His neighbors were pulled
into forced labor. His family was taxed with little left.
The Word of God was ignored, and godly worship was
twisted to do whatever served the powerful.

"Lord, the God who knows us, where are you for
your faithful people?" Habakkuk's heart expressed.

He continues:

> **Why do you force me to look at**
> **injustice?**
> **Why do you tolerate wrongdoing?**
> **Oppression and violence are right in**
> **front of me.**
> **Strife is ongoing, and conflict escalates.**
> **(Hab. 1:3)**

He described the oppression and violence that
smacked him in his face. It escalated, piling higher
and higher, like a mountain that blocks the sun. It felt
hopeless.

"When will it be too much, God?"

Have you asked that? "When will the injustice hit
the point that you have to take notice, God? Do you
even see?" It is as if we are watching wave after wave
pound against a rocky coast at high tide. Set after set of
waves brings in the debris from the ocean and crashes
it against the rocks. Surely as the water level rises, it will
eventually be too much. Surely, it will stop, and the tide

will reverse, shifting and flowing back out. When will it be too high? When will you reverse it, Lord?

Some of God's people in Habakkuk's time were faithful. They were the ones listening in on Habakkuk's prayer time. Others in Judah were anything but—taking advantage of those in need and seeking their own pleasure.

So Habakkuk said:

> **This is why the law is ineffective**
> **and justice never emerges.**
> **For the wicked restrict the righteous;**
> **therefore, justice comes out perverted.**
> **(Hab. 1:4)**

Let's zoom in on this verse. In the first two lines of verse 4, Habakkuk made the claim that the law of God wasn't working. The word for "law" here speaks to what should be ruling the society, the law of the land. It also speaks to God's teaching for his people's spiritual and moral formation. Those who followed Jehoiakim into idol-worship and greed now rejected God's instruction. Their personal make-your-own-religion led them to ignore the practices of the temple, designed to form their hearts and shift how they treat others. What was the impact on justice for the hurting? It never showed up.

With muddied allegiance to the Lord, their devotion to things like the idols of the king brought injustice to the community. Their lack of faithfulness to God led to lack of faithfulness to others.

In the second sentence, the servants of the Lord were surrounded by betrayers, as the word *restrict* literally means "to encircle." Those who cheated and manipulated for their own gain gathered around those who would not give up their integrity, like bullies ganging up on a playground child or a wolf pack enveloping prey. People who should be trustworthy entrapped instead. There was no place to turn. Habakkuk said it again—justice? It was twisted and bent, winding like the country road that gets you nowhere. It's as if the constant reoccurrence of "justice" indicates that it is meant for all mankind.[6]

Isn't this the common pattern of injustice? Those who should have done right have done wrong. Those who should have stood up to stop it didn't. Those supposedly trustworthy instead conspire for their own gain. Just like thousands of years ago, muddied allegiance to God (and to his means of grace that form our hearts) leads to unfaithful care for the hurting. When we become devoted to idols that make our lives easier, like the status-giving idols of Egypt, we are less willing to do what's right for our neighbor.

Do you feel like you're living in that place where you, in some form or fashion, long for the wrong to finally be set right? Do you feel like you looked to those with lots of promises, only to find that the results were twisted versions of the truth with no strong advocate in sight?

---

6. Maria Eszenyei Szeles, *Wrath and Mercy: A Commentary on the Books of Habakkuk and Zephaniah* (Grand Rapids: Wm. B. Eerdmans; Edinburgh: Handsel Press, 1987), 6.

Friend, that's where Habakkuk was living. The wicked surrounding the righteous and justice coming out bent.

If we are meant to live in a just community, then what do we do in the face of the opposite? How do we respond with faith?

Lament like Habakkuk

I was driving alone just a few short blocks, hurrying to a work meeting after a lunch date with a friend. My emotions were so raw; it's seared in my memory. I trembled a bit from the news I'd heard. "God, don't let this happen. God, change this. It's wrong." My prayer wasn't very articulate, but it was aloud and desperate. Decisions were being made that ignored the needs of young ones—destructive decisions. I fiercely wanted to protect but had no control. I drove through tear-flooded eyes and prayed. You've probably uttered similar furious prayers with fresh urgency at a hospital bedside, for your marriage, or for someone vulnerable you knew.

Habakkuk's emotions are at the same intensity. We see it and we *feel* it as we read. He's not holding back, not politely asking a favor with flattery. Instead, he shows us the way to honest prayer when our eyes see evil and our hearts ache. What do we do with the anger, powerlessness, and despair if we pay attention? We lament.

Lament is a plea for help that describes suffering. It declares wrongdoing for what it is—unjust. When you've prayed desperate prayers, you were lamenting in faith. You said what should not be and sought the One who could help. It's not complaining or whining. Following this prophet, it's a bit like a protest. The act of lament reminds us of two things: what is true and right about God and what is true but wrong about the world.

See, Habakkuk assumes we know the truth about God at a gut level. You don't ask God to help and expect him to act unless you truly believe (1) God hates the evil and corruption he sees and (2) the world is revealing its brokenness in injustice. This pain is a result of the Fall, when our first parents chose to disobey, leading to a world in crippling rebellion against God.

Habakkuk knew that God was not one of the idols of neighboring countries, invented by man. The prophet prayed to the Lord, Yahweh, the God who made a covenant with his people, binding himself to them.[7] *He* was the God who made the world in perfect goodness. *He* was the God who had promised blessing through Abraham's family to the world, and *he* declared Abraham righteous by his faith. *He* was the God who had worked miracles to redeem them from slavery in Egypt. God's right law revealed himself as a God who loved righteousness and hated injustice.[8]

Part of lament is deep remembering.

I know a lot of things. I know what temperature to brew green tea and how to cook pancakes. I also know the truth about God's character. I have heard it, studied

---

7. We'll talk more about the covenant God made with the people of Israel in the next chapter.

8. See Exodus 22:22; Leviticus 19:33–34; Deuteronomy 10:17–19.

it, and even taught it. But lament asks me to remember it when fear and anger beat against my mind, like a storm that keeps you up at night. It's not knowledge we access when we are sleepily making breakfast and tea in the morning. It's what we know in distress and desperation.

In those times, you and I may have doubts and questions. Suffering makes the ground under our feet like the shaky bridge on a child's play structure. What once felt solid, now makes us wobble. Lament gives us patience with the complexity of our thoughts while coming to God.

The first truth lament announces to our own hearts and those hearing is that we believe God is trustworthy, even in the crucible. After all, you cry to and with a person you trust. As I said before, lament is an expression of faith.

The second truth lament fiercely declares is that the world is not as it should be. It isn't what we were made for, nor is it what we were redeemed for. We plead for what is moral and creational, asking God to reestablish the "right-order" in the fallen world.[9] Injustice disorients us, as it should.

When I was learning to scuba dive—before most wore a dive computer on their wrist—the instructor told us what to do if we got rattled on a dive. It can be dark

---

9. Mark A. Seifrid, "Righteousness, Justice, and Justification," in *New Dictionary of Biblical Theology*, ed. T. Desmond Alexander and Brian S. Rosner (Downers Grove, IL: InterVarsity Press, 2000), 741.

under the water. Add that you may be diving in caves or at night, and it's pitch-black except for your flashlights. Your senses are baffled, hearing only swishing of water and an occasional tapping or scraping from the fish or your dive buddy. You taste only saltwater and the silicone mouthpiece. If something happens, you get pushed against the coral, and flipped over, you may not know which way is up. In that terrifying moment, take a deep breath from your tank and blow air out your mouth. Watch where the bubbles go; they will always go up. It will always be true; bubbles go up. That is the way to reorient yourself and find your way to the safety of the surface.

So, when injustice flips us over with anger and despair, we look to what's true and doesn't change. God's character—his rightness, goodness, power, his care, his slowness to anger—is always true. The wrongness of evil is always true. Faith in what God has said about himself and lament at the evil we see—this is the way to reorient ourselves. This is the way up. Always.

It is our act of faith in the face of evil: lament.

I taught a Bible study on Habakkuk during the pandemic. Three women in that study of twenty experienced their husbands abandoning them within a few months of our start. Between them, the husbands left decades of marriage and half a dozen confused children, exiting without a word, for a new woman, a new state, or a new vision of life. The women reeling in divorce were in different decades of life, previously unknown to each other, but each grieved with lament. "God, what are you doing? How long until you bring what is right?" They wrestled with what I will easily call injustice—broken covenants. The pain was palpable in our conversations, but their prayers said God's character is true and the world is broken.

Prayer is not idleness when we are faced with injustice. It is engagement. For if our faith says that God is powerful to act, then going to him is the most effective action. If we don't lament, our vision is likely blocked, seeing only the wolf pack, instead of looking up to him who is strong enough to protect and judge.

The grieving prophet models for us how to respond to evil. So we *pay attention* instead of looking away, *lament* instead of numbing out, and *ask* with expectation instead of avoiding God altogether.

Following after Habakkuk

You've probably guessed that this is not the end of Habakkuk's strong emotions about evil. When do ours just come out once? We also haven't heard what God will say in response. Yet we already see Habakkuk's faith lived out. It's tenacious and raw and feels a lot more like my real life than some cliché advice. I'm guessing it's more like yours too.

There's more for us in Habakkuk's journey. But before we move on, let's look closely at his example of paying attention, lamenting, and asking.

Pay Attention

It's easier to leave injustice in our blind spot. This is especially true when the injustice is being done to those with different life experiences than our own, or we cannot see beyond our own suffering.

Yet misuse of power and corruption are alive and kicking, and more are enslaved worldwide today than ever before. When we pay attention, we see the children without families and the desperate refugees searching for safety.

There may be three women in your small group whose husbands just left them. Your neighbor may face prejudice on a weekly basis for his ethnicity. Your friend's children may struggle with anxiety from bullying that shouldn't be theirs. God *sees* the injustice on the grand stage and in small corners—he does not look away. And you know what? He asks his people to do the same.

The call of the prophets begging God to act shifts in the New Testament. God has already come in Jesus Christ and continues to work through his Spirit. So now, we read the exhortation for God's people to be alert and ready. We must pay attention to what is happening around us and to God's work in the world.[10]

Lament

Lament reveals that we've paid attention. It either leaks or gushes heartbreak, questioning, or fear. The

---

10. See 1 Corinthians 16:13; 1 Peter 5:8.

pleas disrupt the guise of ease and happiness in the godly life and reveal pain with which each of us wrestles. It's lived-out authentic faith, shedding light on hurt, giving words to grief.[11]

Following Habakkuk's example means we pray with the range of emotions we see in Scripture, many of which are not evident in the examples in social media stories or inspirational, self-help books. We pray with outrage, disgust, and urgency. Sometimes it sounds like: "LORD, why do you stand so far away? . . . In arrogance the wicked relentlessly pursue their victims; let them be caught in the schemes they have devised" (Ps. 10:1–2).

Lamenting like this forms us. It means that we, like David, can begin with "How long, LORD? Will you forget me forever?" and end with "But I have trusted in your faithful love; my heart will rejoice in your deliverance. I will sing to the LORD because he has treated me generously" (Ps. 13:1a, 5–6). He is imploring "Stop, and stop now, God" when he says "How long, LORD."[12] David expresses real anxiety, agony, and defeat—and yet still concludes that the covenant God will keep his faithful love to him.

Habakkuk's prayer gives us permission to lament *together*, as the church. This can feel strange because I have had people in power manipulate and mock me but

---

11. Mark Vroegop calls it "the grace of lament" in his book *Dark Clouds, Deep Mercy*, revealing how it helps navigate the wilderness of grief. Christianity suffers when lament is missing, he says. Mark Vroegop, *Dark Clouds, Deep Mercy: Discovering the Grace of Lament* (Wheaton, IL: Crossway, 2019).

12. John Goldingay, *Old Testament Theology: Israel's Life* (Downers Grove, IL: IVP Academic, 2010), 215.

never had to worry about abuse that hurt my body nor took the roof from my head. This is not true for all our brothers and sisters. When we speak of lament for injustice in this world, I, along with many in our churches, must see that we do not bear the brunt of it.[13]

So we shake off our pain-averse hesitations and lament together, for the evil that others live under.[14] Habakkuk doesn't ask God to stop the terror for his own sake, he speaks of what he sees happening to God's people around him. So must we.

Ask with Expectation

Watching him closely, we see Habakkuk asked with faith for things to change. He believed God was King and, therefore, in charge.

Remember the story of Peter being put in prison in Acts 12? Herod had killed the apostle James to the anguish of the church and the entertainment of the locals. Herod then arrested Peter for his next demonstration of power

---

13. In Mark Vroegop's second book, he provides valuable instruction on how lament is our right response in racial reconciliation and opens doors for us to "weep with those who weep." Mark Vroegop, *Weep with Me: How Lament Opens a Door for Racial Reconciliation* (Wheaton, IL: Crossway, 2020).

14. "Lament is what happens when people ask, 'Why?' and don't get an answer. It's where we get to when we move beyond our self-centered worry about our sins and failings and look more broadly at the suffering of the world." N. T. Wright, "Christianity Offers No Answers about the Coronavirus. It's Not Supposed To," *Time*, March 29, 2020, https://time.com/5808495/coronavirus-christianity/.

and to the glee of the people. Injustice? Peter was going to be killed for their *pleasure* after Passover.

As Peter was in prison, the church was praying fervently for him.

God miraculously freed Peter! He walked out of prison and arrived at the house where the church was praying for him. When he knocked, Rhoda, a servant girl, came to the gate. In her great joy at hearing Peter's voice, she left Peter—a fugitive who had just escaped death row—outside, exposed. Rhoda tried to convince those inside that Peter was there, but they only questioned her sanity.

The church had prayed with fervor and faithfulness, no doubt, but when the time came to witness their answered prayers, they conjured up all sorts of defenses against the good news that stood right outside the door. They prayed, but without expectation.

We pray, knowing our God is powerful enough to change any circumstance, and we pray expecting him to work. We know he may not work in the ways we foresee, as Habakkuk discovers soon. Still, we look for evil leaders (like Herod) to be thwarted and for the hopeless sufferer (like Peter) to walk free into the arms of the local church who is on their knees.

Lamenting Faith and Jesus Christ

Several centuries after Habakkuk, God, in the Incarnation, descended to answer the laments rising up from the world. In the life of Jesus, we saw the Just One.

Then, the greatest injustice—the death of the perfectly innocent Son of God—brought hope for healing and full restoration. In his suffering, he bore the penalty for the injustice and then rose from the dead. "The resurrection of Jesus is God's own proclamation that he is not far, and that evil will not triumph."[15]

If you cry out "How long, oh Lord?" know that it isn't that God hasn't done anything, but rather that we are waiting for him to finish what he began in Christ's death and resurrection. Our "How long until you act?" is instead "How much longer until we see your righteous judgment permeate our lives?" That is exactly where he is taking this world.

Lament prepares us for hope in God gathering his people to a place ruled fully by his justice, which is precisely where this conversation is going.

15. Tremper Longman and Raymond B. Dillard, *An Introduction to the Old Testament: Second Edition* (Grand Rapids: Zondervan, 2006), 469.

Chapter 2

Faith in a God Who Works

"God, what are you doing?"

"Is it good for you to oppress, to reject the work of your hands, and favor the plans of the wicked?"

Job's question to God (Job 10:3)

Powerlessness is a terrifying feeling. It's worse when you feel powerless and afraid because of people who are supposed to protect you. When leaders show that their own agenda outweighs their care for those they shepherd, the situation turns ugly.

Fear and manipulation from such leaders can bring confusion. Do you remember the fog when trust was broken from someone you trusted deeply? Did you keep asking God what he was doing and, honestly, why he wasn't doing what you thought he should? I sure did.

Perhaps your boss made an unfair decision, or the governing body of the school was the one. The pastor or elder board concluded your claims weren't valid. Or even an injustice in a courtroom where the truth didn't rule. You've asked: *God, what are you doing?*

It's the same question my friend asked God as she wrestled with loss and anger and powerlessness. Her husband left her and her three kids for a mistress with whom he quickly created a new life. He expected little consequences, leaving her to deal with the trashed family stability in the lives of their children. *God, are you doing anything?*

It's the same question a friend asked when another snide comment about his ethnicity hit him while at the store, declaring unequivocally his lesser status. The security guard then asked him his business because he looked "suspicious." *God, are you doing anything?*

It's not an uncommon question. Habakkuk sat in the same emotions. He cried out to God and wondered what he was doing, waiting for his answer. As a boy, Habakkuk learned about God's Word, and what he learned laid a foundation for what he would now hear in God's response.

Habakkuk's Hope for Renewed Repentance

Habakkuk grew up under the reign of King Josiah. Josiah came to power as a child. He was a good king, one of the few "good" kings of Judah. Under him, Habakkuk got a taste of what godly leadership could be like, leadership that led to revival. King Josiah listened to the prophet Zephaniah, who called for a return to the Lord's commands. Desiring obedience to the Lord, King Josiah repaired the temple and found the book of the law (2 Kings 22–23). After reading what was likely the book of Deuteronomy, King Josiah was wrecked.

Deuteronomy includes the final sermons of Moses. It reminded God's people they were the children of Abraham rescued from Egypt and given a law to obey. They belonged to the Lord. As they entered the land promised to their father Abraham, Moses commanded a covenant renewal ceremony. (It's as if they were to renew their marriage vows.) God had bound himself to them and called them to obey, but there was a choice to be made regarding their own faithfulness. Would they choose to obey and live in relationship with God?

If they obeyed, God would bless them beyond what they'd ever seen (Deut. 28). The description of the blessings overflow with wealth, security, goodness, and the world's respect because they bear the name of the Lord. It's a return to the best things of the garden of Eden in the promised land. There are also consequences for abandoning their God, disobeying his law, and worshipping other gods. These covenant curses begin with hardship and disease and spiral all the way to devastation.

The people would end up eating anything they could find and, finally, the Lord would allow another nation to conquer them and take them captive. It's loss, loss, loss. It would have been an awkward renewal party, worse than a drunk groomsman with the microphone, because Moses brought bad news. He knew this hard-hearted people, and the Lord had told him they would choose sin, disregard God's law, and end up with all the curses.

Like the broken compass that keeps pointing the wrong way, they would choose to rebel until they received internal heart-change (Deut. 29:24–28; 30:1–6).

Josiah saw his people in the mirror of Moses's words. They'd followed the path of curses and rebellion. Exile was coming.

So Josiah sought the Lord; he sent men to Huldah the prophetess. Humility, repentance, faithfulness—that's how this king led.

Huldah validated Josiah's fears; exile disaster was coming for the people of Judah, but it would happen after the death of the repentant king (2 Kings 22:14–20). The news was mixed, but Josiah was steadied toward faithfulness. He had read about a covenant renewal party, so he held one. Whatever time he had, he would lead people toward obedience. He read the whole book of Deuteronomy to the inhabitants of Jerusalem and Judah—from youngest to oldest. Imagine young Habakkuk in the crowd soaking in God's law and faithfulness. That's a day you never forget.

Standing by a pillar in the temple, the twenty-six-year-old monarch declared he would follow the Lord and keep his commands with all his heart and soul. "Follow the Lord with me!" Josiah called to the people; they agreed. The king held them to it and removed the idolatrous symbols and places, along with the mediums. He reinstated the Passover for worship, gratitude, and generosity toward the Lord. It is around this time that Jeremiah began prophesying, and King Josiah listened.

When Josiah was thirty-nine, world powers formed an alliance surrounding Judah. The king met Pharoah in battle and was killed. Remember meddling Pharaoh Neco? This brought Judah under Egyptian rule, and Pharaoh put Jehoiakim on the throne as a token king to send him tribute (2 Kings 23:34–35). Josiah's faithfulness and godly courage descended to Jehoiakim's cowardly leadership, corruption, and self-centered gain in a matter of months.

Josiah had been an example to Habakkuk in his youth. He was the guy on the poster beside his bed. Even as Habakkuk cried out to God in the chaos and evil under which he lived, it wasn't as if the people of Judah had never seen good leaders and loving shepherds. They had! King Josiah worked to put boundaries around injustice and idolatry.

Even though warnings of the exile came through Moses, Huldah, and a list of other prophets, perhaps Habakkuk thought there could be another revival and repentance before the conquering army of God's discipline came down like a fist.

There are times when you and I see or sit under wrongdoing, and we pray, "God, do something." We pray for repentance for the evildoers, that their eyes will be opened to the true character of God and the pain they have caused. We pray those we fear would turn into trophies of grace before a watching world and the transforming power of the gospel would be on display. We want a King Josiah to reign again. And sometimes, the Lord does that. The Spirit of God and the Word

of God work together—like they have all through his-
tory—to bring about a repentant and courageous leader.
But many times, that is not what we see the Lord do.
Instead, we sit in Habakkuk's place, and we wait.

The Lord's Response

Sometimes we're so fervently seeking good news,
that we can be caught off guard by the bad. Several
years ago, I was in the ICU after being rear-ended.
Seems like an overreaction, right? I thought so.

By the time I was settled, it was late evening, and
I was convinced I needed to be in my doctoral class
intensive the next day. I begged the physician to plan
my release for early morning. After dropping a few hints
that I did not pick up, he looked at me and told me, with
my brain injuries, I may not be able to walk in the morning. That's not where I thought the conversation was
going. It went from fixing the problem of a missed class
to a terrifying ordeal. From a request for help, to a pronouncement of an overturned life. (Don't worry, though.
I was fine and even made it to class. I was released in the
morning after they figured out someone had misread
my brain scan.)

Our friend Habakkuk lamented the violence he saw
around him in Judah. "How long?" was the familiar cry
in response to the seeming lack of action on God's part.

He was asking for help, and instead, he received a
pronouncement of an overturned life.

We hear God respond:

> Look at the nations, and observe—
> be utterly astounded!
> For I am doing something in your days
> that you will not believe
> when you hear about it.
> Look! I am raising up the Chaldeans,
> that bitter, impetuous nation
> that marches across the earth's open
>   spaces
> to seize territories not its own.
> (Hab. 1:5–6)

God was not passive. He had not been distracted by other things and missed the chaos happening in Judah. No, God answered this man of faith by telling him to look at what he was going to do; God was doing something they wouldn't believe. (Quick sidenote: Have you seen verse 5 on pottery or bookmarks about what God is doing? This verse is about invasion, friend. Don't put it on your knickknacks. There are better verses for that.)

What was this "something in your days that you will not believe"? A Babylonian army God was bringing against Judah. It would cross the nations and take the homes of countless people. In short: an invasion was coming from some of the scariest people they'd heard of. The passage referred to the Chaldeans, which was the name of the ruling tribe in Babylon from the southern region. They were considered fierce, taking charge of their own kingdom, and so their name was used. But make no mistake, these are the Babylonians that history tells us would come and conquer Judah.

As we can imagine, this was not what Habakkuk was hoping for. Yet, having talked about the words spoken to God's people, we know that this shouldn't have been a surprise. It was the result of disobedience. God's response was coming. The insidious impact of sin would now come down on all of Judah—the faithful and the wicked.

That Babylon was coming should not have been a surprise either. More than one hundred years previously, King Hezekiah, one of the mostly-good kings, had shown all the treasures of his house and God's temple to a group of leaders from a country named—you guessed it—Babylon. Hezekiah thought perhaps it would bring about a political partnership, when he should have been trusting the Lord for security. Isaiah responded that Babylon would ultimately sack Jerusalem and take everything Hezekiah had just shown off (Isa. 39:6–7). Thus, here the Lord made good on Isaiah's prophecy.[1] Babylon was coming.

In his dialogue with Habakkuk, the Lord went on to describe the coming Babylonians with metaphors of animals that should make us shudder. We rarely see wolves today, but I can tell you, I have no desire to meet them,

---

1. Isaiah also prophesied that God would use Babylon to punish his people earlier in his book, calling them his warriors to execute his wrath in Isaiah 13. Yet, he also makes clear how he will punish them for their own sins, especially of pride and violence (Isa. 14:1–23).

especially with our young child in my arms. The coming
army was as alert and quick as the wolves hunting at
night. They are also compared to leopards and eagles
(Hab. 1:8)—fast, fierce, and furious. Look at how the Lord
describes them.

> **They are fierce and terrifying;**
> **their views of justice and sovereignty**
> **stem from themselves.**
> **Their horses are swifter than leopards**
> **and more fierce than wolves of the**
> **   night.**
> **Their horsemen charge ahead;**
> **their horsemen come from distant**
> **   lands.**
> **They fly like eagles, swooping to**
> **   devour.**
> **All of them come to do violence;**
> **their faces are set in determination.**
> **They gather prisoners like sand.**
> **They mock kings,**
> **and rulers are a joke to them.**
> **They laugh at every fortress**
> **and build siege ramps to capture it.**
> **Then they sweep by like the wind**
> **and pass through.**
> **They are guilty; their strength is their**
> **   god.**
> **(Hab. 1:7–11)**

The Babylonians had no respect for authority but laughed at kings and walls that would keep them out (Hab. 1:10). The metaphors depict their greed, cruelty, and pride. Finally, it describes their idolatry: "They are guilty; their strength is their god." (Hab. 1:11) They worshipped their own might. What a terrifying picture.

God had heard his prophet. How can we know this? Because God repeated the very words that Habakkuk used for "justice" and "violence" (Hab. 1:7, 9). But he used them to show how this army made their own justice and were coming for violence. "I've heard you, Habakkuk. But it's going to get worse," God essentially said.

The Lord wasn't rationalizing these soldiers as decent men. He was acknowledging from the beginning that what was coming next wouldn't end the violence or bring about final justice. The Babylonians were wicked themselves, but Judah would not avoid this coming covenant judgment. There would be no negotiating, holding on, nor defensive victory. Remember how the Lord referred to them at first? The conquering nation was compared to a hurrying man and bitter herbs. The coming experience was bounding upon them, and it would not taste good.

The God Who Works in Holiness

Are you asking how this could be God's response to Habakkuk's heartfelt plea for help? I get it. Habakkuk asked God to work, and this was not what he meant!

King Josiah's work of reform and renewed faith was not coming back, as Habakkuk hoped.

But even as you and I wait in the face of pain and injustice, sometimes the chaos of judgment is exactly what God is doing. How can that be comfort? Because God is the Judge who is working now, even in mysterious ways, and pointing his people to ultimate justice.

Some of us still squirm and ask: "Can judgment bring good?" Our question may reveal that God values justice more than we do. We want peace, even if that means putting up with some small continual wrongdoing. At times, we want amity and stability, at the cost of integrity and good.

If God judged the corruption of leaders close to us, it would embarrass a lot of people—so it's best if we ignore it, we think. If God exposed the greed and mismanagement of that executive, it could topple the jobs we enjoy, we reason. If God judged a politician for his policies that pad his power but impede justice for the marginalized, it could make our lives uncomfortable, we fear. We wonder if judgment of *those people* is truly good, or even loving. We ask God to be just . . . sometimes. We pray he will wipe out the sin *around* us and not the sin that *benefits* us. Ultimately, we have forgotten about God's holiness.

Holiness is not an aspect of God; holy is who he is through and through, as Jackie Hill Perry has written. "When God loves, it is a holy love. When God reveals Himself as judge, pouring out His cup on the deserving,

He has not ceased to be loving, or holy either. In all that He is and all that He does, He is always Himself."[2]

God always works in a manner consistent with his character. In holiness, God removes disobedient people from his presence. He did this when Adam and Eve disobeyed. They were exiled from the garden. Really, this was God's mercy, for sinners cannot stay in the presence of a holy God. So when God's people in Israel abandoned the law he gave them—the law that called for loving neighbors, protecting the vulnerable, and keeping Israelites from idolatry that ate them like cancer—they, too, were exiled away from the land and the temple where his presence dwelled. God removes his disobedient people, but he does so with a plan to save them and bring them back, just as he did with Adam and Eve.[3] God's grand work of redemption includes discipline grounded in his holiness and just judgment.

---

2. Jackie Hill Perry, *Holier Than Thou: How God's Holiness Helps Us Trust Him* (Nashville: B&H Books, 2021), 15.

3. Paul House sees a structure in the Book of the Twelve (what we often call the Minor Prophets) that shows Hosea through Micah warning God's people to repent, Nahum through Zephaniah (where Habakkuk falls) as dominated by the punishment for lack of repentance, and Haggai through Malachi focusing on hope of renewal, forgiveness, and restoration. This structure helps us understand the emphasis of the Lord as Judge in Habakkuk and less emphasis on renewal, though there are mentions of it. We read the Bible as a whole and in context. Paul R. House, "The Character of God in the Book of the Twelve," in *Reading and Hearing the Book of the Twelve*, ed. James D. Nogalski and Marvin A. Sweeney (Atlanta: Society of Biblical Literature, 2000).

It's easy to forget that God's holy character is also slow to anger, as he told Moses. He is a God of grace and compassion, of faithful love and truth. He forgives in his faithful love, and he also will not leave the guilty unpunished in his justice (Exod. 34:6–7). God doesn't lose his temper and lash out without patience, like you and I do. And yet, consequences had mounted over hundreds of years on a people who had broken his covenant. The history of God's people in 1–2 Kings shows that the people had put themselves under the warned curses. And God does what he said he would do.

How is this good? When my daughter was small, she would often ask the same questions on repeat: "Who are you? What's your name? How old are you? What are we doing today?" She knew all the data about her parents, but she wanted to hear again who we were and what we said would happen. (This could backfire when plans changed, and the preschooler wanted predictability.) God has told us who he is and what he will do. The exile reveals a holy God who is constant. He works to keep his covenant and discipline his people. *This is good.*

All that Israel was tempted to trust would be stripped away, like a detox program; the promises of their God alone would be left. Isaiah describes it as burning away the dross in discipline (Isa. 1:25–26). He would bring his remnant back to the land and give them the leaders who make justice happen, those who lead in righteousness. God's faithful love wouldn't stop working for his people—just as Deuteronomy told King Josiah and Habakkuk.

The God Who Works for Us

In Deuteronomy, when Moses told the people of Israel that they would break the covenant, end up with the curses, and be exiled, he also told them God would restore them to the land. And God did bring back a remnant of his people to Judah after a time, but the prophecy Moses spoke included more—a multiplication of the people and internal heart change, things that didn't come at the return of the land (Deut. 30:3–8).

Moses was referencing a greater restoration; Jeremiah and Ezekiel joined in about this coming new heart just a few years after Habakkuk. They spoke of a New Covenant to come, where God would cleanse his people and change their hearts to want to obey him (Jer. 31:31–33; Ezek. 36:24–32).[4]

Isaiah echoed the prophetic chorus, saying the Lord's servant would one day take judgment for his people's sins (Isa. 53). This Servant brought the New Covenant and an internal heart change we desperately needed.[5]

---

4. The themes of exile and restoration provide guidelines for understanding the provision of Jesus Christ. It is at the cross that the full punishment is taken by the Messiah himself. He was the Suffering Servant who took the punishment of exile we deserve in his death. His restoration came in his resurrection and ascension to the right hand of God. We who have faith are united with him and given the benefits of his restoration. Yet we continue to wait for the full restoration with the complete fulfillment of the reign of the Messiah following his return (Acts 3:21). Read more in O. Palmer Robertson, *The Christ of the Prophets* (Phillipsburg, NJ: P&R Publishing, 2004), 501.

5. See Luke 22:20; Hebrews 9:15; 2 Corinthians 3:6–18.

We may question if God works for us, you and me, and he has. We know salvation from greater judgment is possible for all, for those trusting in the Lord in Habakkuk's day and in ours. Though you and I deserve to be removed from God's presence as sinners, in Christ, our judgment has fallen on him instead, and he transforms our hearts.

Still, sometimes our lament to God is answered with more suffering, even suffering that prunes. What he's doing may feel confusing or infuriating, but God has not taken a vacation and left us to flounder on our own. His devoted love for us hasn't changed because of our wrestling, and while it can be hard to feel that the work of Jesus shows his love for us today, it does.

When we call out to him to do something in our country, our world, our families, and our ministries, and what happens is not what we wanted—God is still working.

God may bring a hard blow of judgment against the wicked, toppling nations. God may discipline his people, rocking a church, exposing a leader, bringing hardship on brothers and sisters (Heb. 12:3–13). Other times it's not discipline but only suffering allowed, and after self-examination, we cling to God who loves us. Have you seen him discipline to strip away all other supports? Or seen him allow suffering that causes us to cling to what he has said? *Even then, God is working.*

God's declaration of judgment to Habakkuk doesn't easily answer all the questions. The fear and confusion didn't fade, but only escalated. How can this be the way? That's exactly the question the prophet asked next.

God, What Are You Doing?

Unpretentious Habakkuk reacted with emotions of dismay, but first he acknowledged who God was and what he had heard.

> Are you not from eternity, LORD my
>   God?
> My Holy One, you will not die.
> LORD, you appointed them to execute
>   judgment;
> my Rock, you destined them to punish
>   us.
> (Hab. 1:12)

Remember when God said, "You would not believe it"? Well, Habakkuk can hardly believe it. He begins by calling on the Lord, the everlasting God who is holy. He's the Rock who has stabilized them, referring to the song Moses sang at the end of Deuteronomy (Deut. 32). Habakkuk speaks God's character as if to remind himself and God who he is.

Then, he leans on what else he knew from Moses. God has ordained these Babylonians for judgment. And still he echoes his refrain of "injustice" because of the seeming contradiction in the Lord's character and this plan. Look at verses 13 and 14.

Your eyes are too pure to look on evil,
and you cannot tolerate wrongdoing.
So why do you tolerate those who are
treacherous?
Why are you silent
while one who is wicked swallows up
one who is more righteous than
himself?
You have made mankind
like the fish of the sea,
like marine creatures that have no
ruler.
(Hab. 1:13–14)

Habakkuk asserts: *Wait, God. You are pure and holy.
You wouldn't do this. Would you use people who are more
evil than us to punish?* *You control all things, and these
guys are horrible and destroying the world. How could you
be silent while a wicked person takes out the righteous?*
Remember that Habakkuk is a prophet who isn't speaking from God to the people, but right now he speaks
from the people to God. He speaks for those who are
righteous in Judah, those who are surrounded by the
wicked (Hab. 1:4). *What about the faithful, God? Do you
see them?*

God, you have made us vulnerable, he says next. His
argument declares mankind like the fish of the sea without a ruler. *You made us to be taken advantage of like this,
God* (Hab. 1:14).

His prayer turns to the abusive, idolatrous actions of the Babylonians. They are like ruthless fishermen. *It's like they throw nets to catch and kill people, and then they worship the net. They worship their killing mechanisms, God!* Habakkuk expresses (Hab. 1:15–17). For all they care about is indulgence and pleasure. They are merciless. It's as if Habakkuk wants to provoke God's righteous anger against them as well as against the unjust in Judah.

I may not describe those around me as fisher-men, but there are some who seem to be hippos. These placid-looking and strong animals rule the rivers in many countries. They eat only grasses and as such would seem safe and pleasant to admire and live around. Yet they are the most dangerous large animal in Africa—aggressive, territorial, and known to crush people. Leaders such as these can seem strong and safe, but instead are controlling and crushing to God's people, doing whatever it takes to protect their territory and power. Like Habakkuk, I have prayed: *God, as we have prayed for growth in your kingdom, how have you allowed these people to lead? Why give them power?*

And what about the faithful sufferers, God? Why do people get the consequences of the sins of others, just as those who were faithful in Judah received? As I write, another story is spreading virally across the Internet. Details of a bully pastor and the devastating impact of his ministry. Community lost. Faith of new believers shaken. The pain from the testimonies is gut-wrenching. It can be tempting to go right along with the worst of these leaders if it gives us the life we want, seeing the growth and excitement. We may end up idolizing the evil mechanisms, like the nets of the Babylonians, if it makes us feel good. I may not call us fish like Habakkuk does, but I ultimately agree with him; we're vulnerable to the unscrupulous leader who comes to take power.

Have you asked with me: "What about the sufferers caught up at no fault of their own, Lord?" Habakkuk feels the tension between what God will do and God's character. He understands the coming exile, but *how is this the way to do it?*

So Habakkuk stations himself like a guard on a watchtower waiting for the Lord to respond (Hab. 2:1).

Praying like Habakkuk

Habakkuk's outburst doesn't feel like a model prayer in the Bible. His appeal erupts with questions and dissent. I'm so glad that we're never called to stuff our emotions; we can bring the confusion, grief, and protest to God, even if it gets fiery.

It's wonderfully clear that God can take it. Countless people in the Bible have asked similar questions as sufferers, waiting on God, looking at his character and what they saw around them. God heard them—Jeremiah, Job, David, Naomi, Habakkuk—and in no place in this section do we feel that God chastises his prophet for his questions or complaint. As one commentator put it: "This intensive probing of the purposes of God by the prophet should not be analyzed as a manifestation of weak faith. Both the nature and purpose of God elicit from the prophet expressions of confidence. Not a weak faith but a perplexed faith torments Habakkuk."[6] Faith that trembles with confusion or protest is robust faith.

So as God welcomed Habakkuk, he welcomes you and me when we know he is working but disdain the way it's going. Anyone's prayers get heated? Mine do. I want to pray like Habakkuk, but I also realize there is a temptation to attempt to demand from God. How do we pray with such honest anguish and grief like Habakkuk and not turn our request into an attempt at bending God to our own will?

Habakkuk is bold, but not pompous. He's not trying to manipulate God, like sacrifices were designed to do to pagan deities. Nor is he leaving God his "review." Prayer is not an evaluation of God, deciding if he is found wanting, like the loser of a reality show who is asked to leave. It may be heated, emotional, and a protest, but if it's like Habakkuk, prayer reveals devoted relationship and not hubris. Habakkuk is the friend of the honest doubter who will humbly speak to God instead of just about him.

There will be times in our lives when we, like Habakkuk, will see what is happening around us and ask God: "How does this match with who you are?" Doubts may come, just like rain does with the storm. Still, our walk of faith means we come to him. Like the family member who has done something that has you furious. You cool down and realize you need to talk it through.

---

6. O. Palmer Robertson, *The Books of Nahum, Habakkuk, and Zephaniah*, 2nd edition (Grand Rapids: Eerdmans, 1990), 157.

You can express your hurt, even with emotion, because you are in a trusting, safe relationship that you know isn't going anywhere.

At the end of our prayer, even if we don't have answers, God wants us to know that he is the God who is working. As one late professor and minister said, "God is always at work, always involved, always pressing forward toward his Kingdom. But the means by which he chooses to pursue that goal may be as astounding as the destruction of a nation or as incomprehensible as the blood dripping from the figure of a man on a cross."[7]

God Is Doing Something You Can Believe

Waiting for final justice doesn't end in the days of Habakkuk, nor the exiles, nor those who returned to the land of Judah. The question of "God, what are you doing?" and his response, "I am working, even if it's a way you do not understand," reverberates through history.

Paul spoke of this very thing to the synagogue at Pisidian Antioch in Acts 13.

First, he told them of the familiar story of God's people—the Exodus, the Promised Land, and Kings Saul and David. You can imagine the crowd smiling and agreeing with their beloved history. Perhaps with a deep breath,

---

7. Elizabeth Achtemeier, *Nahum—Malachi: Interpretation: A Bible Commentary for Teaching and Preaching* (Atlanta: Westminster John Knox Press, 1988), 38–39.

Paul transitioned and told them from David's descendants, God had brought the Savior Jesus! Though killed, God raised him from the dead, like he promised their ancestors (vv. 30–32).

I'm guessing the smiling and nodding had stopped, but Paul didn't. He quoted the Psalms and Isaiah, showing how Jesus's resurrection fulfilled the Scriptures. Then, he said it. There was hope for those who failed to keep the law of Moses, hope for the once-exiled and returned people of God who *continued* to fail at lawkeeping. Forgiveness and being made right with God were offered through Jesus (vv. 38–39).

Did they hope? Did their minds run to the promises of the prophets? Were they furious at what Paul implied he knew?

Some responded the latter, as Paul closed his sermon by quoting God's message to our friend Habakkuk.

> So beware that what is said in the
>   prophets does not happen to you:
> "Look, you scoffers,
> marvel and vanish away,
> because I am doing a work in your days,
> a work that you will never believe,
> even if someone were to explain it to
>   you."
> (Acts 13:40–41)[8]

---

8. The quotation here doesn't match exactly what we see in our Bible in Habakkuk 1:5. That's because Luke, the author of Acts, is quoting the Septuagint (LXX), the Greek translation of the

"Will you believe what God is doing?" Paul warns. It may look like a crazy thing—even the opposite of what you wanted with a shamed, dead man of low status offering forgiveness to the entire world—but God is working.

Just like Habakkuk wrote for his day, the Jews would face surprising judgment if they didn't respond and believe in Paul's day. Their only hope was dependent faith—now a humble faith in the work of God through Jesus Christ, the way to life.

We will ask at times: "God, what are you doing?" but we *know* that he is doing a work in our day, revealing the resurrected Jesus, just as Paul said he was doing. So we cling to Christ's judgment-taking death, and we go on believing that God will do what he said he would do, even if things get harder before they get easier. It's long-haul faith that waits.

Habakkuk wrestled and protested in the misery of waiting for justice. It's the normal human experience to wrestle with what we see. Yet God doesn't leave Habakkuk in his wrestling; he has more to say. How do we wait with faith? God's answer to the prophet centers our entire Christian hope.

Old Testament with some abbreviation and a slight change. Luke believes that God is doing a work again that provokes the unbelief of the Jews and renders them liable to judgment. G. K. Beale and D. A. Carson, eds., *Commentary on the New Testament Use of the Old Testament* (Grand Rapids: Baker Academic, 2007), 587.

Chapter 3

Faith in the End

God: "There is a way to live."

*"It is not in the nature of things for him who is
to live, to live otherwise save by faith."*

John Chrysostom, fourth-century
archbishop of Constantinople[1]

Earlier, I told you that after college I moved to Eastern Europe. God had called me to serve on a ministry team that shared the message of God's character, love, and redemption to a people who had seen his name used to defend war crimes.

After living there for a few months, my roommate and I realized one day that we needed to get our friend to a doctor. We were turned away at a medical clinic,

---

1. John Chrysostom, "Homilies of St. John Chrysostom, Archbishop of Constantinople, on the Epistle of St. Paul to the Romans," in *Saint Chrysostom: Homilies on the Acts of the Apostles and the Epistle to the Romans*, ed. Philip Schaff, trans. J. B. Morris, W. H. Simcox, and George B. Stevens, vol. 11, A Select Library of the Nicene and Post-Nicene Fathers of the Christian Church, First Series (New York: Christian Literature Company, 1889), 349.

so we drove through the city, frantically searching for another option. Finally, we left our beat-up junker with two wheels on a curb, blocking a third of the street, so we could hobble up a hill with our friend's arms over our shoulders. We honed in on the unmarked building at the top of the rise we had been told was a hospital. When we reached it, the doors were locked. Pounding with my fist, I yelled the words for help as loudly as I could.

Medical personnel finally answered the door. They found three young women, exhausted. Teary eyes and a pounding heart didn't help my novice use of their language. I tried to say, "We need help. My friend is sick. Blood. Help. Please."

After deliberation, suspicious nurses led us to a small exam room. Someone who I can only assume was a doctor came in for a few minutes. An hour passed, and they sent us home, shocked and scared, not wanting to leave. My friend would only live another day.

The needs were left unmet, and then questions flooded my mind. What had happened? Why was there no help? Why would we be turned away? *How are we supposed to survive in this world with so little stability, God?* Though I didn't read Habakkuk's words at the time, I expressed his sentiment: *God, you've made mankind in chaos!* (Hab. 1:14).

We didn't know at the time that my friend had a condition no hospital could have treated. No medication or procedure would have changed the outcome. Still, the experience of being led out of a hospital when we knew deep down we needed to stay stuck in my mind. It wasn't right, and I had no power in the situation. What hope does God give us to live in such a world?

Begging for an open door, for help, for a better answer is not my unique experience. It may not have been a pounding fist against a physical door, but many have been turned away and asked the question of how to survive in a world such as this. In a family that hurts those it claims to love. In a broken system that punishes those who are trying to do good. In a society that cheers more fighting, apathy toward the afflicted, and selfish gain as the goal. We have more than desires; we need justice.

Habakkuk's Journey of Questions

Remember, young Habakkuk watched good King Josiah rule. Josiah had ordered the upkeep of God's temple, and when they were doing the cleanup, they found the "book of the law," likely the book of Deuteronomy (2 Kings 22). Josiah lamented at what he heard in the book and read God's Word to the people. It would change the entire society.

Habakkuk grew up under the tutelage of Deuteronomy. It was *his* book of the Bible, like the one you may have colored, underlined, and reread in your early days of faith. But Habakkuk's opening lament reveals his questioning God's Word. Does the law of God do what it should—does it stop wickedness (1:4)? His prayers brought new questions. After hearing God's answer of coming judgment, he then questioned how

the holy God he'd read about could tolerate the treacherous Babylonians.

Our doubt of God's Word pops up in our own wrestling. "God, but you said . . ." has been heard in many
a prayer. Where is God's favor on his people when
Afghanistan falls to the Taliban and his church flees for
their lives? How is God leading his people "beside quiet
waters" when division splits his people to the point of
church families being ripped apart? Where is the "grace
of the Lord Jesus with us" when one group oppresses
another for a leg-up and control? Habakkuk wants to
know how to live in such a world, because it does not
match what he's read in his Bible.

Injustice underlines the instability of the world and
throws us into surging questions of what we know.
Incredibly, the wrestling believer is cared for and never
demonstrated as a nuisance.[2] Habakkuk shows us God
isn't distant or apathetic and never dismissive in our
search for hope. The King of the World is listening.

Still, in his next response, God doesn't defend himself or pull back the curtain on his entire plan, just like he
didn't for Job. Instead, the King looks that resolute man

---

2. Habakkuk was revealed as a partner and companion of the
Lord God. This is especially true of the prophets in this sec-
tion of the Book of the Twelve, meaning Nahum, Habakkuk, and
Zephaniah. The thoughts of God himself are shared with the
man, and he speaks in partnership with what the Lord wants
to reveal, especially in what's coming next in Habakkuk 2:6–20.
For more on this, see Paul R. House, "Dramatic Coherence in
Nahum, Habakkuk, and Zephaniah," in *Forming Prophetic Literature*
(Sheffield, UK: Sheffield Academic Press, 1996).

on the watchtower in the face and leans close. It's as if he tenderly acknowledges the pain and disorientation Habakkuk has felt and gives him instructions for how to live in the midst of dissonance.

The Lord's Instructions

Before Habakkuk heard from the Lord, his expectation must have been high. He wanted answers and hope. Have you leaned in with anticipation like that?

The Lord's reply doesn't resolve all anxiety and confusion. There were no charts revealing how God could use evil people. Instead, the Lord gave Habakkuk what he truly needed—two commands and a vision of hope.

> **And the LORD answered me:**
> **"Write the vision;**
> **make it plain on tablets,**
> **so he may run who reads it.**
> **For still the vision awaits its appointed**
>   **time;**
> **it hastens to the end—it will not lie.**
> **If it seems slow, wait for it;**
> **it will surely come; it will not delay.**
> **(Hab. 2:2–3 ESV)**

God was going to give him a vision, a message, but first, God had two things for him to do. What did he tell him?

Write it down.

How important is this message? So important that it needs to be inscribed. When else were God's words written down on tablets so it would last? Your mind may be thinking about Moses on Mount Sinai, the covenant with Israel and the Ten Commandments, like mine is and Habakkuk's was.[3] Habakkuk knew God was about to tell him something significant, and the news must spread. *Make the writing legible,* the Lord said, *so people can read it and run to tell everyone.* This is news for the way to live!

Imagine what it was like to wait for news of hope in those days? In early fall during the COVID-19 disaster of 2020, the forests of Oregon where I live erupted in flames. Communities I love evacuated, and firefighters rallied as hazardous smoke covered the entire state. One volunteer fire department told the story of being trapped. After days of fighting heavy smoke, high winds, and raging fires, there was no way out for a mountain town in the middle of the forest. The highway to safety was blocked in both directions by boulders and downed burning trees. They abandoned all structures and belongings to focus on preserving life. In desperation, the firefighters began to move the seventy trapped

---

3. Other prophets wrote on a book or tablet, but only Habakkuk uses the plural which is elsewhere used to reference the law. Additionally, only is the law commanded to be written very clearly, like it says here in Habakkuk 2:2. (Isa. 30:8; Exod. 24:12; 34; Deut. 9:9–10; 27:2–3, 8). See Rikki E. Watts, "'For I Am Not Ashamed of the Gospel': Romans 1:16–17 and Habakkuk 2:4," in *Romans and the People of God: Essays in Honor of Gordon D. Fee,* ed. Sven K. Soderlund and N. T. Wright (Grand Rapids: Wm. B. Eerdmans, 1999), 7–8.

community members to the docks of a mountain lake for a "last stand." Just imagine them on those docks. Then news came. Messages from the Forest Service reached the firefighters—they had found an evacuation route on forest roads. No forest ranger was keeping that news to themselves; this was the way out of disaster. The good news flew to those watching the flames. This is the way to live, they said.

The Lord God was giving Habakkuk a way to live, and the faithful people of Judah waiting for their corrupt society to be judged desperately needed it.

We need a way too. Like those trapped and standing on the dock of a lake, we're watching injustice burn life around us, and we need to know the way to live in this world of instability.

The Lord told Habakkuk to write it down, and then he gave Habakkuk a second command.

Wait for it.

The Lord knew that waiting had been the current vocation of the prophet. God's faithful people had been waiting on God's promises for generations; they'd longed for the descendant of David who would bring real justice and righteousness (2 Sam. 7:12; Isa. 9:7). Now before God even told him the vision, he prepared him to wait—again.

It's something that happens at the end, he said. *Don't give up. It will surely come,* the Lord assured his people repeatedly. You can trust in what I'm about to tell you. Even when a cruel tyrant was coming by God's own hand to overtake the land, he was their faithful God. Yet his timing was not the same as what Habakkuk wanted.

Justice deferred haunts us. We want God to give answers and to be the judge *today*. Some days he does that, like the man in my newsfeed today who was released from a jail after serving for a crime he did not commit.

So when God spoke to Habakkuk, it's as if he was speaking slowly and leaning close. He acknowledged the waiting and the pain in waiting. Patience feels like salt in the wound when you're waiting for justice. But the vision was the way through all you see, God said.

It's as if we've marched up a hill here alongside Habakkuk, with our complaints about injustice flowing as we climbed. We've stood at the top trembling with anger, weariness, or confusion, and like the watchmen, we've waited. Here's the view that will help us see and live.

The Vision of Hope

The vision arrived:

> "Behold, his soul is puffed up; it is not
>   upright within him,
> but the righteous shall live by his faith."
> (Hab. 2:4 ESV)

How is this the exalted vision of hope? Who are the puffed-up? Who are the righteous? What does this mean?

Let's break it down. Trust me. It's worth the lead-up.

Look, the soul that is proud and puffed up cannot be upright. God reminds Habakkuk what matters in the end—those who are right before him and those who aren't. The puffed-up look to themselves for justification and will find none. They will not stand before God.

The Lord sees the arrogance of the invaders, and they will have their own judgment in time (Deut. 32:43). But this isn't just about the Babylonians. By not naming them, God's reminding us that he is the just judge over every proud tyrant. The holiness of God that Habakkuk declared in his last prayer isn't out of date. The evil we see in the world will not be ignored by the righteous God. It may not come in our lifetime, but it *will* come in the end. The proud and doers of injustice will not stand.

But for now, the righteous shall live by faith.

Who are the righteous? Habakkuk used the term "the righteous" in his first prayer; it's those who still worship the Lord and don't understand how God and his covenant have left their society in vicious turmoil. They are the loyal who look to God for hope.[4] If you're reading this book as a follower of Jesus, God is talking about you, you who are looking to him for hope in the midst of chaos. You, brother or sister, live by faith.

---

4. Ezekiel, a contemporary of Habakkuk who wrote a bit later in Babylon, referenced the righteous as those who follow God's statutes and act faithfully. This person will certainly live, the Lord said. This clarifies who the righteous are and affirms Habakkuk's message (Ezek. 18:9).

Now, the phrase "live by faith" has been stitched on enough pillows to fill a city and drained of its real meaning. Its depth has turned into fluff, meaning something like "just keep believing good things will happen." Out of context, the statement is incapable of holding us in a storm and is only a powerless saying, resembling the fill of the pillows it covers.

Yet Habakkuk's whole conversation has culminated in this. It's finally an answer to the internal question of how to live in the face of injustice and coming further injustice. The one surrounded by the wicked like a pack of wolves (Hab. 1:4) can live. He or she can survive by faith, not faith in the universe "bringing good one day." Rather, faith in the Lord God who has a covenant with them and faith in what he has said will happen in the end.

Will this faith help them live through this moment of utter chaos? God says it will. *Faith in a just, faithful God who gives life is how you survive chaos,* he says. *And it's how you stand in the end.*

This is the panoramic view from the heights—final justice for the evildoers and life for God's people of faith. Do you see it? I know the church has looked out of touch when they've said injustice will be judged, and they've said it as the flames got closer. This may feel tenuous for a suffering Christian trying to hang on after questions, doubts, and grief. But God isn't asking us to pull off faith on our own. He is reminding his people who he is when he is asking for faith. Let's look closer at the words in Habakkuk 2:4.

The Faithful, Just God

Remember Habakkuk's favorite book of the Bible, the one King Josiah found—Deuteronomy? In it, Moses wrote down God's law and urged the people to listen to it, and toward the end of his life, he sang a song. This is the song we can assume Habakkuk recalled when he called God his Rock.[5] Maybe it was playing in his head as he prayed. Here's part of the lyrics:

> For I will proclaim the LORD's name.
> Declare the greatness of our God!
> The Rock—his work is perfect;
> all his ways are just.
> A faithful God, without bias,
> he is righteous and true.
> (Deut. 32:3–4)

When the Lord gave a vision to call his people to faith, he chose his words carefully. The words in Habakkuk 2:4 are ones tied to Moses's song in Deuteronomy 32. The Lord is the faithful one, the same word for faith in Habakkuk 2:4. The Lord is the righteous one, more so than we are. The Lord is the true one—literally "upright"—even

---

5. Moses, in his song, calls the Lord "the Rock" five times (Deut. 32:4, 15, 18, 30–31). The song also progresses to predict the disobedience and idolatry of God's people, their punishment through an enemy nation, and the vengeance of the Lord on the enemies, ultimately purifying his land and his people. Habakkuk was likely thinking about this song, affirming the Lord's faithfulness as their Rock, even as he will judge (Hab. 1:12).

if the proud aren't, Habakkuk argues. "All his ways are just," the song sings.

It's as if God hints at the song Habakkuk is humming, telling his questioning disciple, "You may not understand all my ways, but my word is still true. My character still as solid as a rock. On this you can place your faith."

This song of Moses goes on to speak of the discipline God will bring on his people when they rebel. He will also judge their enemies, it says. The Lord is doing exactly what he said he would do; it's all in keeping with the covenant that Habakkuk grew up hearing and which changed his life. The Lord's Word is trustworthy—even when suffering fills the horizon.

You and I hear God's vision of hope—judgment for the prideful unjust ones and life for the loyal with faith. It may be hard to absorb or see as relevant.

So we sing with Habakkuk that God's character hasn't changed. We sing when we *want* to be full of faith and know God is faithful to us. And when we *want* to believe in justice and know that God will bring it one day. We sing that God is true and upright, even when the bullies of the world are not. We sing when we know that God sees our suffering. I bet Habakkuk kept humming it.

Faith doesn't mean we don't suffer, or deal with trauma, seek counseling, or fight injustice. The consequences of injustice are still dire. Friends, like mine, may still die. Bullies may still win. (More on this in the next chapter.) Habakkuk's people who were sitting in the midst of an oppressive government were awaiting invasion.

Faith means that in the insanity of banging your fist on a closed door and asking for help and justice, there is a way of endurance, lifting our eyes to what will happen in the end. It is the vision of the final judgment where every act of oppression will be judged. The proud, self-reliant will not stand, but we can because of our faith in a just and faithful God.

When my daughter went to her first soccer class as a three-year-old, there were twelve small children chasing balls, laying on the field, and throwing cones. When the coach came up and asked her to dribble the ball across the tiny field to shoot it into the net, my daughter just stared at her. The coach urged her with one of their learned mantras: "Say, 'I believe in myself!'" My daughter looked her in the eye and deadpanned: "I believe in Mommy." I laughed. I couldn't dribble the ball much better than she could, but we can understand what she was doing. Someone was asking her to do what felt impossible, and the person standing in front of her was downright scary. In her panic, she wanted out of the terrifying scene, and she knew who could bail her out—Mom.

Our situations of injustice are sinister and dangerous. I don't mean to downplay that, but her statement has been echoing in my head. When we don't know the way out, living by faith throws ourselves on the One who can deal with the circumstances. We don't have faith that we can bring justice; rather, we have faith in One who can.

The Feel of Faith

The word *faith* is embroidered on plenty of décor as well. For some, those items may honestly remind them of faith in a powerful God, but for many it's a buzzword that is supposed to make us feel better on a bad day. Habakkuk would have thrown such an item against the wall.

Even as Christians, we often think of faith as something we conjure up in our heads, like a formal statement of assent we'd provide in court. Yet the Bible uses the word *faith* differently. The Hebrew word ties us into an understanding of steadfastness, trustworthiness, and honesty. It is a congruence between what you say you believe and what you do. To live by faith is to hold firm, when all else falls away, just like the society that crumbled around Habakkuk's neighbors.

On our cold and windy Oregon coast, the sand is blown into high dunes in some towns. You can stand out on one of those dune ledges with a beautiful view, but you'll also feel the ground slither out from under you if you're not careful. The sand collapses right off the cliff with enough weight. But if dune grass and brush have grown, you're safe, even on the edges. The roots provide your feet a stable platform, even in the extreme gusts. Faith in the Lord is like the roots that don't move, even if you're afraid you may fall.

Faith isn't stoicism or resigned apathy toward suffering and injustice. Nor is it naïve optimism and ignored doubts and questions.[6] This world really is as steady as a choppy wind blowing to knock us off our footing. Yet faith is the firm attachment and belonging to the covenant God, and thus loyalty to him, even in the gale. It's faithfulness that fleshes out as obedience—even in suffering.

In the summer of 2020, an explosion near the port of Beirut rocked the city. The day is vivid in my memory because I was leading an online cohort of Middle Eastern female leaders through a hermeneutics course, several of whom live in Beirut. Seeing the headlines that day, I left my family playing on the beach to get on my phone and hear if my sisters were alright.

The blast was one of the largest nonnuclear explosions in history, injuring 7,000 and displacing 300,000 people. Documentation revealed the Lebanese government had been knowingly storing nearly 3,000 tons of ammonium nitrate in a populated area. Many leaders knew the danger; they did nothing. My Lebanese friend was supposed to be meeting with her pastor at their church when the explosion occurred. The church was leveled in the blast.

By God's kindness, plans had changed, and instead, she was at home where her windows blew out. She survived without injury to care endlessly for the traumatized in the coming weeks and months. The words out of her mouth, even in continued corruption, violence,

---

6. D. A. Carson, *How Long, O Lord?: Reflections on Suffering and Evil*, 2nd edition (Grand Rapids: Baker Academic, 2006), 70.

economic crisis, health struggles, and tears were: "Thank God for his protection and his sustaining grace." No accountability has come on any Lebanese leaders. And the faithful sisters and brothers I know don't expect any. They are focused on the ministry of the church, even though my anger at the injustices toward them still fumes. They know how to live in such a world where God will surely bring justice in the end.

Look again at Habakkuk 2:4, this time in another translation:

> **Look, his ego is inflated;**
> **he is without integrity.**
> **But the righteous one will live by his**
>   **faith.**

It is telling that the call to live by faith is in contrast to the way of the self-reliant, one with an inflated ego. The proud have no integrity because they decide for themselves what is true and live for their desires. While I'd rather self-identify with the righteous, the pull toward pride and self-ruling fills our culture. My social media feeds are littered with influencers preaching to me that I have what it takes and can do whatever I put my mind to. We want to rule our own worlds by our own will, neglecting the need for obedience and loyalty, as if we stick it in the drawer with the sweaters that no longer fit the trends of the day. Yet the faithful? We must decline the invitation to self-reliance every day to live by faith.

It's not a new struggle. One preacher almost fifteen hundred years ago taught through Habakkuk and said,

"[Pride] suggests to them that they are great, that they need nothing, that whatever they do, think or say is all due to their wisdom and their prudence . . . they seize the glory of God and offer themselves to be admired in his likeness."[7] It's as if he knew about the subtle and not-so-subtle self-promotion we do online.

Whether it is intellectual ability, status, economic comfort, career accomplishment, or even the perceived skill at the Christian life, if any competence of your own holds your confidence for happiness and security, that's not faith in the life-sustaining and life-giving God. The claim of self-dependence and glory becomes even more enticing when we suffer, for we can attest our survival and moral judgment is due to our own strength rather than God's power and revelation. But living by faith cannot be playing God.

In the face of pain and fear, faith often feels like the next steps of faithfulness and humble dependence. It's not flashy, but rather doing the things needed for today—loving the people before me, choosing obedience instead of expediency, believing his Word, and like the righteous did in Habakkuk's day, trusting what he will do in the end.

7. From Martin of Braga (fl. C. 568–579), an Anti-Arian on the Iberian Peninsula. Quoted in Alberto Ferreiro, ed., *The Twelve Prophets*, OT Volume 14, Ancient Christian Commentary on Scripture (Downers Grove, IL: IVP Academic, 2019), 189.

The Hope of the End

When we stand like a watchman, asking God how he could allow such injustice, the answer he gave his prophet is for us. He tells us to wait for it.

He tells us to look to the end—the unjust arrogant will be judged, and his faithful people will live. It's a reorientation in the midst of affliction because of what we can see. Isn't that what we observe God-in-the-flesh do with Martha? Martha greets Jesus with heartbreak and faith in John 11 after her brother died. Emotional, she declares that Jesus could have kept him from dying, and she knows God gives him what he asks for. Even in her grief, she looks to him for hope, just like Habakkuk.

Jesus tells her: "Your brother will rise again" (John 11:23), and she responds with faith in the end—resurrection on the last day. But Jesus shifts her perspective from general belief in the last day to faith in the One who rules that day. "I am the resurrection and the life. The one who believes in me, even if he dies, will live. Everyone who lives and believes in me will never die" (vv. 25–26). He asks her if she believes. I imagine she sighed as she leaned her faith into him as the life-giver and the way to resurrection. She says she believes. He is the Messiah, the Son of God for whom they have waited.

Death still stung. She didn't know that Jesus was going to raise her brother that very day. But her faith grew to a confidence in the way God was going to give life to his people of faith—through Jesus Christ.

Sitting in my apartment praying with a numb and angry heart about the death of my friend and the instability of the world, I remember the Lord drawing me to this story of Martha and Jesus. In the grief, God wasn't asking me to forget the injustice and brokenness of the world. He didn't ask for an abstract belief of an end. Instead, he leaned in and asked if I believed what the Scriptures testified to. He asked, in essence: "Do you still believe that I bring resurrection and life and that I will do it through Jesus?" It didn't eliminate the pain, but it reminded me of what is still true. I responded, "Yes, Lord," as I stared out the glass doors to the ridiculous non-balcony. It felt brave to say it out loud to the empty room. "Yes, Lord, I believe that Jesus is the One." In believing, I knew my friend may have died, but she will live. And one day all things will be made right.

Christ leads us into the way of life, but not because death isn't horrendous and this life is reliable. Jesus still wept at the tomb of his friend and mourned the power of sin and darkness in the world. But he brought Lazarus back from the dead and then went to the cross—bearing injustice—so that Lazarus, you, and I could live without forever death. If only the upright make it in the end, we can live by faith and stand before God in the end, because Jesus *makes* us righteous and upright. It's our dependence on Christ's work that will save us. Just as Habakkuk heard the familiar words of Abraham's given righteousness by his faith when he heard the vision of Habakkuk 2:4, so this vision from the Lord sets the stage for the way of salvation through Jesus Christ.

Living by faith is at the core of the gospel, as Paul quotes Habakkuk in Romans 1:17. Paul says that the righteousness of God in a person is revealed from faith; that faith is its origin and its direction.[8]

At the end of time, we will come to the final stages of redemption, and God will wipe away every tear from our eyes, as if acknowledging all the pain of the fallen world's claws (Rev. 21:4). His justice, righteousness, faithfulness, and trueness of which Moses sang will saturate our lives and those of everyone there. Of course, death will be gone. Grief, crying, and pain won't exist because their sources are gone (vv. 3–4). The character of God floods the crowd, healing in his presence. Faith in this tomorrow is how we live through the instability of today.

Faith in the End, Still Evil on Earth

When our questions are unanswered or additional suffering is next on the schedule, just like Habakkuk, this is where God leads us—to faith that looks forward to things being made right again and a faith that acknowledges evil still plays on earth. This is what we see from the heights of God's vision for Habakkuk.

My cross-country coach in high school walked every racecourse with us. Through the muddy trails and forest (think Oregon rural rainy autumn), he taught us to find

---

8. Robert Mounce, *Romans: An Exegetical and Theological Exposition of Holy Scripture* (Nashville: Holman Reference, 1995), 73.

the glimpses of the finish line between the leaves, even if we had another loop on the trail to go. *Always look to the line, every chance you get,* he'd say. Toward the end of the race, when we were depleted, we knew where we were going, and it sustained us to the end. We live in an unstable world by believing what the Lord says about the finish line. We look there every chance we get. It's the view of the horizon that changes our prayers.

Still, the chaos of the earth hasn't subsided. It didn't for the faithful of Judah either. Just after the call to faith, the Lord reminded Habakkuk that the Babylonians are still coming. In Habakkuk 2:5, he says that their drunkenness, arrogance, and greed will bring them driving toward the nations, like a harvester taking all the fruit he wants. He never has enough, always taking more, like death itself. No acknowledgment of approval, this is a recognition of the teeth of injustice that continue to destroy and an indictment of coming judgment.

So, to my friend in debilitating pain, who is accused of being a druggie looking for another fix because of a doctor's prejudice—you, sister, may the Lord lift your eyes to the end as you live by faith.

To my friend who saw his parents and the foster care system fail him over and over growing up, only to work hard and still find mental and financial stability hard to retain—you, brother, may the Lord give you faith in his faithfulness.

To my friends denied health care for their daughter because insurance won't cover the surgeries needed from her genetic condition—may the Lord bring justice and give you and your child faith to survive.

To brothers and sisters in Afghanistan, unknown to us, but known by God, who are waiting daily to see if you will live—we hear the stories of your faith, the gospel from your mouth to your attackers and your ministry to your neighbors. May you be reminded of the life-giving God and the life of faith.

INJUSTICE AND JUSTICE

Chapter 4

Faith Under Oppression

"God, people are terrible."

*"The horrors of our times call for complete justice—
justice which the world can give only in part,
but which the gospel provides in whole."*

Kori Porter, CEO of religious freedom
advocacy organization, CSW-USA[1]

No one could hide Emina[2] and her family, so they packed what they could carry and fled for the border in the middle of the night. Multiple armies moved through the Bosnian countryside at the time, each one putting a different set of neighbors at risk for their lives. Emina's family thought there were mass graves just down the road, and the changing rumors of which militia approached the village produced constant panic.

---

1. Kori Porter, "How to Live When Justice Is Partial," in *His Testimonies, My Heritage: Women of Color on the Word of God*, ed. Kristie Anyabwile (Charlotte, NC: The Good Book Company, 2019), 128.
2. We will call my friend "Emina," though that is not her real name.

That night the intel put Emina and her family in jeopardy, and though they had hidden others, no one would hide them.

Emina's family fled further and further north, to the most northwestern part of the neighboring country, where we both lived, as if distance could heal the evil experienced.

So we were walking side by side on a sunny, normal day many years later, when Emina's lips released her story of desperate flight from the coming army. This time I wasn't hearing a story of war refugees from a history book, detached and surrounded by dates and people groups I could not keep straight. It wasn't on the news. It was my *friend*, flesh and blood, walking next to me up La Guardia street in Rijeka, Croatia. It was Emina who lived around the corner and who joined our Bible study who had fled ethnic cleansing and systematic mass rape. I knew she was Bosnian, so there were assumptions that could be made in the early 2000s. The war had ended not that long ago. The war crimes from that conflict were still being litigated at the International Criminal Tribunal.

She told me her story about how she had fled from their Bosnian hometown. The impact of the trauma weighed heavy on her, and she saw it on the faces of her parents daily. The violence done in the name of religion, for the sake of power, radically changed her life. The city where I lived housed crowds of Balkan people who fled violence. Their stories made the abuse of those in power all the more real.

You may have never wandered a city with a friend who told you about their narrow escape from a violent mob. Though perhaps you have. The stories of my international refugee friends who have come to Oregon are not dissimilar to this one.

The scars from damaging abuse don't mark only those who have survived war. Many of us have hidden scars from abuse that we consider less dramatic. When those in power took and did what they wanted and left wreckage behind.

The painful experiences we've suffered (or those we've watched others endure) naturally unearth questions about accountability. Who can do anything to stop the powerful from abusing the powerless? Where is the strength to endure? How can we live by faith under oppression?

Through the centuries, power has been misused, and people have cried out to God about it. When we last saw Habakkuk, he was receiving a vision from God that was to be recorded and anticipated. It was a vision of the ultimate status of the proud abusers—an end that left them hopeless in their self-dependence.

Even as the vision closes, the reality of the horror of the Babylonians resurfaces. Yes, God has promised the future demise of such an enemy, sure, but *right now*, they are on the move, and their impact on God's people will be severe. They are coming fast, and there is no way out. How does God expect his people to endure and live by faith in the face of such news? God's next reply communicates that *God's people endure by hope in what God will do*. They endure because God will judge.

The Lord's Gift of a Mocking Song

God's subsequent response to Habakkuk is the gift of a song. It may not appear like a gift at first glance, like a present that comes in a paper bag instead of beautifully wrapped with ribbon, but this song will buoy God's people.

It's a woe song, a refrain about consequences for sin and the need to repent. The word *woe* marks the stanzas of the song, like the beating of a drum, to emphasize the warning. In the song, you'll hear five stanzas of disaster, like boulders following each other in an avalanche, falling on the powerful. The intense imagery would make any reader shudder. Yet trust me; while the song is rated R, it's not the horror film we turn off for fear of nightmares. It's the song God's people would sing when their lives felt like a nightmare, but they knew their God was not only still with them, but that he was going to work. Living in a chaotic world, we need to hear the woes.

Introducing the song, the Lord tells Habakkuk: "Won't all of these take up a taunt against him, with mockery and riddles about him?" (Hab. 2:6a). In other words, "There are indeed victims of Babylon's violence and treachery, but eventually those very victims will turn around and sing mocking songs over Babylon with a taunting lyric like this . . ." God is saying the evil won't get away with what they've done. They will go from high to low, from honor to disgrace, the lyrics chant. The tables will be flipped—a coming reversal.

This wasn't new. God's people had heard God would take vengeance on his adversaries. It was in the song of Moses Habakkuk already quoted (Deut. 32). It was in the covenant with Abraham—the Lord would curse those who curse his family (Gen. 12:3). It was promised all the way back in Eden—a coming Savior, born into Eve's lineage, would crush the head of the serpent so that the power of sin and death would be utterly defeated (Gen. 3:15). Yet the prophet's words remind them there is hope in a God who judges.

Though the song is never explicitly about the Babylonians, the insult and threat ring through, applying to the coming conquering army. Still, it's also for any other abuser. God is helping his people remember, with easily memorized rhythm and metaphors, so this song would echo across fields and long roads as the burdened people worked, waited, and trembled with faith.

The First Verse: The Selfish Thieves

The first verse of the song begins like this.

> **"Woe to him who amasses what is not his—**
> **how much longer?—**
> **and loads himself with goods taken in pledge."**
> **Won't your creditors suddenly arise,**

and those who disturb you wake up?
Then you will become spoil for them.
Since you have plundered many
  nations,
all the peoples who remain will plunder
  you—
because of human bloodshed
and violence against lands, cities,
and all who live in them.
(Hab. 2:6b–8)

Here's the first of the "woes," a word that assures coming judgment on someone. It's not a wish or a feeling or a dream. It's a pronouncement. This *is* coming down the pike. *It's going to happen.*

Consequences are coming for him who has taken what isn't his. The coming Babylonians stole from the people. It's as if the victims were giving loan after loan against their will. But God is saying that in time repayment must be made, hence the imagery of pledges and creditors.[3] The loss was wearying to the point that the singer bursts out in the middle of the song, "How much longer?" mirroring how Habakkuk began this book.

---

3. Do you see the pattern of the song? It begins with a description of the sin (Hab. 2:6), then the punishment (2:7), and finally the reason (2:8). You can see how the last verse of each stanza begins with either the word *since* or *for,* except for the final line (2:20). This translates the same Hebrew word and often reveals the grounds for the punishment. Several of the following stanzas follow this same pattern.

So what will happen? Those "giving" the money will arise and take it back, because the thieves have killed and pillaged. The plunderers will get plundered.

Picture the loss of your property as you struggled to survive, the greedy and merciless taking what you need, by force, manipulation, or "asking for help" in such a way that drains the resources to the dregs. Or, perhaps you don't need to imagine it. Perhaps you've been there—taken advantage of and left desperate. The debts feel huge with no way out, no matter how hard you try.

When I read these lines in Habakkuk, I think of my friend's parents who used the names of their children on financial accounts and lines of credit, leaving the children to discover unknown debt and no ability to rent as they entered adulthood. I think of another friend who is about to lose his house due to a parent's greed and deception. I think of pastors in China who, when not arrested, are being fined exorbitant amounts just for being pastors. (One pastor and his wife received a notice that they would be charged more than $30,000— an amount that would put them into bankruptcy.)

Who do you think of? The Lord is telling us in his song that one day the thieves will experience the loss that they have caused, reaping what they sowed.

It feels strange to sing a song about people being looted in some sort of retributive justice. How is that right? But the singers aren't threatening retaliation, like we hear in some fiery breakup song. The lyrics declare what *God* will do, specifically what he will do to a people at large. Those who heard the song from Habakkuk would not rise up to get justice for themselves; they were going into exile. Yet, one day, the Lord would bring someone to punish the Babylonians as a nation. Revenge is not the comfort for God's people, but the fact that he will judge the unjust for their own deeds. The plunderers would stand not before their own pitchforks, but before Judah's God.

God still judges today those who take advantage of others. The gang who destroys the stability of a neighborhood and the family member who takes until there is nothing left will face him. They may not see consequences in our lifetime, or they may. Regardless, they will stand before God. One commentator calls the world "inherently self-destructive,"[4] meaning God's wrath is expressed in the outworking of the wicked's own actions. Yet God's action against wrongdoing isn't only general and broad, like that coming for the Babylonians. It is also personal and focused; just think of Eli's sons or Ananias and Sapphira (1 Sam. 4:11; Acts 5:1–11).

God sees those who would treat his demand of right action as just another suggestion for their life rather than the rule of the King. This is the promise of verse one: the Lord will take away the gains of the merciless and selfish.

---

4. J. Alec Motyer, *The Prophecy of Isaiah: An Introduction Commentary* (Downers Grove, IL: InterVarsity Press, 1993), 109.

The Second Verse: The Greedy Bully

The song narrows on exploitation: What about those who get wealthy on the backs of others? What about the greedy company leaders who work their employees on the lowest possible wages, leaving them desperate for longer hours to make ends meet? What about the banks that have chosen predatory lending on the vulnerable simply because they can?

Maybe you've felt like you have been used as a stepping-stone for the advancement of others and felt cheated and lied to. Habakkuk sings this song for you to know that God is the judge. He will bring justice.

While the Babylonians were neither literal employers nor lenders, they are pictured as the greedy bully. Here's the second verse of the song.

> **Woe to him who dishonestly makes**
> **wealth for his house**
> **to place his nest on high,**
> **to escape the grasp of disaster!**
> **You have planned shame for your house**
> **by wiping out many peoples**
> **and sinning against your own self.**
> **For the stones will cry out from the**
> **   wall,**
> **and the rafters will answer them**
> **from the woodwork.**
> **(Hab. 2:9–11)**

The unjust Babylonians worked so that their own would have it good, as one who lives large in a safe tower or a nest, while the others below have less and less, barely surviving. Sound familiar? One goes up as he swindles those who tumble down.

But what will happen? Shame. Shame will come to his house. This doesn't feel like much of a punishment to us, as we often think of shame as just a private, individual emotion to process, yet this is a public, society-wide disgrace, like those who lost in battle. It's humiliation and brokenness—what you may have felt when you were taken advantage of with no recourse. *It's the reversal coming, people of faith.* As much as the power-hungry have tried to protect themselves, ruin will still find them, the song says. Even the wood and stone of the house will cry out against them. The savage get shame.

It's the financial swindler, the preacher who tells you God will bless you if you give more money to their ministry. The news just ran another story of a church leader conning the elderly congregation out of their retirement accounts. The shiny new jet and lavish mansion will call out against those leaders for the injustice.

It's a verse for those who have gotten stuck in our criminal justice system unjustly. It's for those who find themselves incarcerated for longer than appropriate and for those who never deserved it, like innocent Philadelphian Curtis Crosland, who was released after

thirty years in prison for a murder he didn't commit.[5]
Curtis isn't alone; 132 people were exonerated in 2021.[6]
This verse is for the innocent who are manipulated.
It's for those who spend years awaiting trial and those
acquitted after they've lost all they had. People beat up
by wrongdoing can sing of a God who will work justice.

But God's song isn't only against greedy bullies.
Next, God sings doom over the violent.

The Third Verse: The Violent

> **Woe to him who builds a city with**
> **bloodshed**
> **and founds a town with injustice!**
> **(Hab. 2:12)**

Who builds their empire on blood? Who controls
and manipulates with threats of violence to build their
sphere, career, ascent to greater power? Politicians may
come to mind. Or you think of organizations that rule by
ignoring vulnerable lives or by covering up abuse only
to breed further wrong. Still others have seen the loss

---

5. Sahar Akbarzai, "Philadelphia Man Convicted of Murder Is
Freed by Evidence That Was on File for More than 30 Years," CNN,
accessed February 17, 2022, https://www.cnn.com/2021/07/31/us/
curtis-crosland-philadelphia-murder-exoneration/index.html.

6. The Root article reveals that of the 132 exonerations, 81 of
them were black. Noah A. McGee, "Wrongfully Accused: The
Exoneration of Black People," The Root, December 31, 2021,
https://www.theroot.com/wrongfully-accused-the-exonera
tion-of-black-people-sl-1848254629/amp. Find more informa-
tion at the Innocence Project, Equal Justice Initiative, and other
organizations.

of loved ones because of an alliance of people designed to terrorize.

Being a punching bag for the brutal is the experience of many in our world. Some of them may be refugees who are your neighbors. Likewise, our brothers and sisters in China report beatings that come along with the common arrests of pastors or house church members. Or maybe you've been on the receiving end of cruelty you felt on your body. Pain, fear, and anger reverberate from the actions of these violent people. It's understandable that we would ask: "Who will hold them accountable?"

> Is it not from the LORD of Armies
> that the peoples labor only to fuel the
>   fire
> and countries exhaust themselves for
>   nothing?
> (Hab. 2:13)

Yes, it is the Lord who promises that people will wear themselves out only to gain nothing but burnt ashes in the end. Like the plans that slip through their fingers, they earn futility. The reversal occurs again; the brutal get a blaze. In case it hasn't been explicit so far in the song who would bring this judgment, it is the "LORD of Armies"—the Lord's "fighting name," if you will.

Let's pause for a minute. Maybe you've been hanging on with me this far, but you're already questioning: *Is this really where our hope lies? Do God's people endure only in hope that God will flip the tables one day?* You're right, friend. That's not the only thing God will do, and our hope lies in more than his just judgment. Look at what our song says next:

> **For the earth will be filled**
> **with the knowledge of the Lord's glory,**
> **as the water covers the sea.**
> **(Hab. 2:14)**

Do you know what the Lord gets when he works his plan to completion? The spread of his glory. The opposite of shame and ashes. We'll come back to this in chapter 6, but for now, we exult in the way his work brings such assurance and good. *We hope in a God who judges, who saves, and who brings his glory.*

The violent are no match for the Lord God. The next stanza makes this even more clear. He's not done offering comfort and fuel for endurance through his coming justice.

The Fourth Verse: The Cruel

> **Woe to him who gives his neighbors**
> **drink,**
> **pouring out your wrath**
> **and even making them drunk,**
> **in order to look at their nakedness!**
> **You will be filled with disgrace instead**
> **of glory.**
> **You also—drink,**
> **and expose your uncircumcision!**

> The cup in the LORD's right hand
> will come around to you,
> and utter disgrace will cover your glory.
> (Hab. 2:15–16)

I cannot imagine singing this verse in church, but God puts the words into his people's mouths to say "the cruel will not escape."

The imagery in these lines is intense. Habakkuk describes the cruel forcing another to drink, mixing in wrath, and making them drunk in order to take advantage of them.

The description is terrifyingly close to sexual assault, which has been a consistent part of ancient and modern warfare and subjugation.[7] The metaphor points to the Babylonians subjugating their neighbors through manipulation and shame, as the people felt helpless.

This topic can bring back traumatic memories, for which I am deeply sorry. God hates sexual assault. He will judge it. Full stop. He will also judge those who manipulate, harm, and shame the vulnerable, as the metaphor sings.

Strategized shame is weaponized by those who want to have control. It can look like attacks on your personhood, oftentimes in the form of accusations that offer no ability to respond. The boundaries of true dignity

---

7. Some commentators believe the original rebuke included calling out such assault. Or it may be a metaphor for the shame the invaders wanted to intentionally bring on the people of Judah.

inherent in a person are ignored like speed limit signs, blown by in full disregard.

We cannot read this and not think of the ways shame and violence have been used in the United States. In 1964 Fannie Lou Hamer stood before a national convention in Atlantic City, New Jersey, and courageously retold her story of attempting to register to vote in Mississippi as a black woman. After losing her job and her home, she was arrested by police. She listened to the beatings and screams of her friend until it was her turn. One prisoner was forced to beat her until he was exhausted, only to have a second assigned to continue the torture. The white police officers beat her head if she screamed and then sexually assaulted her.[8]

That is the evil that God condemns here, and the words of the song are meant to meet us in pain and suffering as they paint a picture, dark as it may be, of poetic justice. Our revenge isn't promised, but God's action is. He will exchange their power for disgrace, at the end, if not during our lives. Fannie Lou Hamer saw tastes of God's power working to bring change, but the accountability for each was still to come.

The lyrics get edgier, as if the people of Judah sing to an audience of Babylonians who function in the lyrics as

---

8. Though her speech did not give her party seats that year as hoped, just four years later Fannie Lou Hamer went on to be the first African American to take a seat as an official delegate at a national-party convention since the Reconstruction, and the first woman ever from Mississippi. Maegan Parker Brooks and Davis W. Houck, eds., *The Speeches of Fannie Lou Hamer: To Tell It Like It Is* (Jackson: University Press of Mississippi, 2010), 63–65.

"you." *The cup in the Lord's right hand, referencing God's fury, will be passed to you. You will have to drink it. There's no way out through your familiar methods of manipulation. You'll go from glory to humiliation,* it says.

The end of verse 16 says "utter disgrace" will come upon their glory. The term for utter disgrace is literally "vomit." In the way alcohol makes some vulnerable, now the attacker will be vulnerable and covered in his own vomit. The cruel will receive God's punishment and any status they believe they have gained will be covered in what disgusts us. As the plunderers will get plundered and the savage will get shame, the vicious will get vomit.

When your eyes cannot lift from the ground and your hands shake because of memories of shaming, Habakkuk's verses want you to hear that God hasn't ignored your pain. When your anger rages at those who have been cruel, he wants you to know that the disgrace and contempt thrown on you will come around served by the hand of the Most Just One as they will stand before him. God's song of poetic justice gave endurance to his people and can again today.

Ironically, later down the line, Babylonian royalty thought it would be a good idea to party with the Lord's cups from the temple. Moments after drinking from them, the infamous handwriting on the wall sealed the Babylonian empire's fate (Dan. 5). The cup of God's anger did come for them.

The Fifth Verse: The Idolators

The final stanza of the song speaks of the self-deceived in idolatry. Foolish false worship fueled the plans of the powerful, and it was out in the open for mocking. We'll look further at their warning and judgment in the next chapter.

Yet the passage makes clear: the Lord doesn't need to be awakened. He is the living God—holy, sovereign, seeing, speaking. He is well aware of the actions of the wicked and rules from a throne in his true temple.

God's song is a balm for the wounded. We sing the verses and end with a vision of the faithful and almighty God who reigns.

Wait, Is God's Judgment Really Comfort for Today?

Can we really believe a song about God's poetic justice coming against abusers? It feels far-fetched in a world where abuse stories run in the news each week and many shrug. And is endurance because of coming consequences on those who harm us too harsh of a concept for civilized people? Isn't it wrong to relish the fact that doom awaits anyone—even the worst of us?

This is not the work of the "Old Testament God," as if he is any different than the God of today. The same holy God is revealed when Jesus preached about judgment and hell, when Paul cursed enemies of the gospel, and when God consoled his church with the words of his vengeance (Rom. 12:19; Rev. 6:9–11). God will bring his punishment on those who choose to take advantage of others today, just like he said he would in the seventh century BC.

Our understanding of God's anger, his wrath, is often tainted by our experience of unjust human vengeance and an over-sentimentalized view of God's love. For "a love that does not contain hatred of evil is not the love of which the Bible speaks."[9] Rather, God's wrath is the just outflow of his love and holiness, revealing his opposition to evil. He wouldn't be loving nor holy if he acted like an apathetic parent to broken cries of his children, or to the turmoil of his creation.[10] Yes, real evil has been committed, and we need a just God who judges.[11] This is comfort for us, according to Habakkuk.

On another sunny day in Eastern Europe, my Croatian sister in Christ told me her war story—her father marched

---

9. Tony Lane, "The Wrath of God as an Aspect of the Love of God," in *Nothing Greater, Nothing Better: Theological Essays on the Love of God*, ed. Kevin J. Vanhoozer (Grand Rapids: Eerdmans, 2001), 139.

10. Joshua M. McNall, *The Mosaic of Atonement: An Integrated Approach to Christ's Work* (Grand Rapids: Zondervan Academic, 2019), 154.

11. Tim Keller describes people who don't want a God who judges. He says they "want a 'God of love,' but a God who does not get angry when evil destroys the creation he loves is ultimately not a loving God at all. If you love someone, you must and will get angry if something threatens to destroy him or her. As some have pointed out, you have to have had a pretty comfortable life—without any experience of oppression and injustice yourself—to not want a God who punishes sin." Timothy Keller, *The Prodigal Prophet: Jonah and the Mystery of God's Mercy*, 1st edition (New York: Viking, 2018), 125–26.

away from their home for execution because he was half Serb, the people group who initiated genocide in the Balkans war. With no conversation, his mixed ethnicity was a death sentence from the angry locals, and a school-aged girl came home to no father. We grieved. We still lament. And we say that the Lord will bring just judgment. When my Bosnian friend Emina spoke in desperation of the traumatic impact of the war on her parents, who struggle to do their daily tasks, we hurt together. We mourn the wounds from fleeing as refugees, from the threat of torture, from the betrayal of neighbors. And we acknowledge together that the Lord God has seen it all.

Paul quoted Habakkuk's favorite song of Moses—Deuteronomy 32—when he reminded the church how we respond to injustice. Don't avenge, he says, God will. Instead, do good to your enemies to conquer evil (Rom. 12:19–21). A Croatian theologian came face-to-face with this when his pen famously wrote of lecturing on the Christian attitude toward violence, his feet resting on land soaked with the blood of the innocent in Croatia. The listeners of his lecture had their cities plundered and burned, had seen brothers killed and sisters raped. Still, he instructs, not to retaliate. He tells them (and us): "Soon you would discover that it takes the quiet of a suburban home for the birth of the thesis that human nonviolence corresponds to God's refusal to judge."[12]

---

12. Miroslav Volf, *Exclusion and Embrace: A Theological Exploration of Identity, Otherness, and Reconciliation*, 1st edition (Nashville: Abingdon Press, 1996), 304.

The faithful living through the war zone will decide to not retaliate not because God doesn't judge, but because he does.

Retaliation isn't the way of God's people, but rather faith in a God who will work—*for deserved consequences and for undeserved salvation*. Remember, we hope in a God who judges, who saves, and who brings his glory.

Esau McCaulley reminds us that the biblical songs that call for judgment against exploitation and terrorization, like the imprecatory psalms and this song in Habakkuk, are places for anger, but they also transform anger. God must judge sin, but the prophets point God's people to the hope of established justice through One who will reconcile warring parties. Lament isn't just for God to right wrongs, but the prophets call the exiled to go further. They were to do something the world would call impossible: look for salvation for their former enemies (Isa. 2:2–5; 49:6).[13] Isaiah, in particular, does this while also looking forward to Babylon's destruction. This is the tension in which we walk. For God's people endure by hope in what God will do—his judging *and* his saving work.

So, we pray for judgment, and we pray for repentance and salvation of the unjust, that as the costly atonement covers us, it may also cover them. We pray for the terrorists who have stolen children in

---

13. Esau McCaulley, *Reading While Black: African American Biblical Interpretation as an Exercise in Hope* (Downers Grove, IL: IVP Academic, 2020), 128.

Afghanistan, those who have gained by treating people unjustly in the United States, and those who killed the courageous believers in Nigeria.[14] When injustice tents over our days like the clouds that never break, even then we follow Paul's command of kindness, Jesus's command of loving our enemies, and the hope that we can conquer evil with good (Rom. 12:19–21). God still uses kindness for transformation and saves people. This is our hope of endurance—God's work of judgment and God's work of salvation. Remember the Chinese ministry couple who was fined enough to send them into poverty? The wife wrote that she wanted to despise the staff at the Religious Affairs Bureau when she set up the hearing date, but the Lord convicted her. Instead, she chose to show kindness, even offering her prayers for them. "If my heart is filled with anger, bitterness, and self-righteousness, then my heart is actually resisting God. Lord, have mercy!"[15]

Black Christians in America have been profoundly influenced by the themes of forgiveness and the community of all ethnicities that fill the Scriptures, though African Americans have faced the abuse, oppression, plundering, and forced manipulation that fill Habakkuk's

---

14. In 2021 Nigeria is where the most Christians died for their faith. Tim Dustin, "The Top 5 Trends from the 2022 World Watch List," Open Doors, January 31, 2022, https://www.opendoors usa.org/christian-persecution/stories/the-top-5-trends-from-the-2022-world-watch-list/.

15. Little Ai, "We Do Not Have to Worry," China Partnership, accessed December 8, 2021, https://www.chinapartnership.org/blog/2021/7/we-do-not-have-to-worry.

song. McCaulley points out: "We have found our way there by means of the cross."[16]

The call to love enemies does not validate continued abuse. It does not mean we do nothing while we are hurt, do not seek justice, or do not hold people accountable. The Lord sent Nathan to rebuke powerful King David for his murder of Uriah and abuse of Bathsheba. Now the Lord's telling his people to sing condemnation over those who would harm them. In the New Testament, James tells us to help the widow and the orphan, echoing the commands of the prophets to defend those in need (James 1:27; Isa. 1:16–17; 58:6–7; Amos 5:15, 23–24). Sometimes that means defending the vulnerable we see in the mirror.

Faith in chaos means trust in coming justice, kindness for those who don't deserve it, honesty about evil, and prayers for unearned grace.

Endurance and Faith

Bullies, tyrants, and the greedy continue today, on the small stage of our homes and on the world stage. You've seen them. There will always be "the Babylonians" in our midst until the final judgment.

So let me tell you what a shepherd of the early church wrote in the book of Hebrews about this.

The author of Hebrews knew of the pressures and suffering facing his believing friends and wanted to urge

---

16. McCaulley, *Reading While Black*, 129.

them toward a persevering faith. It's as if he tells them, "Remember what God told Habakkuk."

He says,

> So don't throw away your confidence, which has a great reward. For you need endurance, so that after you have done God's will, you may receive what was promised.
>
> > "For yet in a very little while,
> > the Coming One will come and not delay.
> > But my righteous one will live by faith;
> > and if he draws back,
> > I have no pleasure in him."
> > (Heb. 10:35–38)

Do you hear him? *Keep going, so you can receive what God promised.* He quotes Habakkuk 2:3–4. *The promises of God may have seemed far off to God's people on the verge of conquest in the time of Habakkuk. And now, when it feels hard and those you love are in prison, we may feel that the promises of God through Jesus Christ are far off. But they're not.*

Bank on your faith, church. The promises will come. Do not throw off your confidence in the great work of Christ. He won't delay. He will come again at just the right time and bring us into the kingdom of justice and righteousness. We're living in the tension of the "not yet," thus the need for perseverant faith in what

God and the writer of Hebrews knows *promises* sustained God's people before us. That's why the words of Habakkuk launch us into the hall of faith.

The list of saints in Hebrews 11 shows that resilient faith is possible, even in the face of shame and death. It speaks of Noah, Abraham, Sarah, Moses, and more. The mothers and fathers of the faith model that if they can walk through alienation, suffering, and delay with faith, so can we. The faithful neighbors of Habakkuk who were going to sit through oppression waiting for justice knew this same path.

When we tell stories of God's work, we must tell stories not just where suffering ended, but where endurance didn't. Sometimes, oftentimes, we don't see the final word on the issue. We don't see the final work of God's promises, even full justice. When we ignore these stories of resilient faith, we forget the Lord is present in comfort and steadfastness in the midst of the suffering as well as the miracle of ending it.

Facing shame, social alienation, and death is exactly what our Savior did. The writer of Hebrews concludes the stories of the faithful with a call to "lay aside every hindrance and sin . . . run with endurance." Jesus went before us, and he faced death and shame and now is seated at the right hand of God (Heb. 12:1–2). Jesus's way to glory was through suffering, and his people follow the same path.

God in the Flesh

The prophecy of the woe song came true. After Judah was conquered, the Babylonians fell as well. But oppression and abuse didn't stop. It continued in the corrupt society of Judah after they returned to their land and when Israel was ruled again by other nations. When Jesus Christ came, there was still abuse and manipulation and pain, but Jesus came to bring true freedom. He took the pain and torture and punishment and rose from the grave.

Those of you who have sat under oppression, who have been abused and asked the questions: "Who will hold them accountable? What hope do I have?" Habakkuk sings a song from the Lord who raises his hand and says, "I will hold them accountable." He will. You may not see it, but they will fall under the weight of their own sin or the weight of their sin will have fallen on Jesus. Either way, the sin will come into the light and be dealt with, and accountability will be fully achieved.

So, while we walk in chaos, we cling to a w faith. We pray, "Come, Lord Jesus," and we know that we are praying for him to bring final justice. In those words, we are also praying for him to work today to save.

If such is true, then we live and wait by perseverant faith; we also tremble at the realization that we have added to the chaos of this world. By faith, we are willing to pay attention to our own greed and use of power for our own good and the detriment of another. Because this woe song wasn't just for comfort; it was for conviction too.

Chapter 5

Faith to Repent

"God, I am terrible too."

"False gods destroy and devour lives, health, and resources; they distort and diminish humanity; they preside over injustice, greed, perversion, cruelty, lust, and violence. . . . Only the gospel exposes the cancer of idolatry. Only the gospel is good for people."

Christopher J. H. Wright, Old Testament scholar[1]

Those of us who were old enough to not be sheltered from the news remember where we were on September 11, 2001. That morning, I woke early and drove into town just as the sun began to illuminate our green country valley in rural Oregon. Being on the West Coast, much had already happened, and my radio was making indiscernible announcements. Confused, I turned it off. I pulled into the women's addiction recovery house where I was babysitting for the week. It was

---

1. Christopher J. H. Wright, "Here Are Your Gods": *Faithful Discipleship in Idolatrous Times* (Downers Grove, IL: IVP Academic, 2020), 97.

in their community room where I began to grasp what had happened. The TV played the video of a plane hitting the tower over and over. A toddler played in my lap. The room began to weep.

The women sitting next to me had lived through their own pain and exploitation; they were survivors. They gathered around the news coverage and asked each other (and eventually the college kid trying to distract the small children in her care) if it was the end of the world. They'd faced their own sin and its impact. Now they were watching disaster on TV. The evil of some destroying others led them to believe the apocalypse had begun. Their next question: *If this is the end of the world, will God's judgment come on me?*

It may sound strange, but their question is not a poor one. Jesus even references a disaster to move us to take account of our own lives (Luke 13:1-5). We read in Habakkuk the condemnation of the Babylonian oppressors and bullies in general. The coming disaster is supposed to bring up questions. If God is judging *them*, what will *we* face if we have harmed others for our own gain?

The Selfish Neighbors

When we read harsh condemnations from a prophetic book, we nod along with disapproval for the "people like that" and sometimes blindly continue in the ways we perpetuate such harm. God's people, even back to Abraham's family, were supposed to be righteous and just and speak up for the vulnerable.[2] They were oppressed in Egypt and were not to treat their neighbors that way. Yet they slid into taking advantage of others, ignoring the repercussions. And, friend, it's an easy pattern to follow.

In the days of Habakkuk, the upper class in Judah shamelessly robbed and exploited the common people, partnering with the corrupt religious leaders. King Jehoiakim only encouraged the injustice as he, too, conscripted slaves to build his new homes and infrastructure. To call them selfish neighbors may be an understatement.

When Habakkuk provided this song for the faithful to repeat, the barbs of accusation snagged the Jewish nobles who heard it. The coming army wasn't the only perpetrator of oppression—the wealthy people of Judah were living just like their selfish, violent foreign enemies. The Lord knew it and provided a song ambiguous enough to provide comfort for his vulnerable people and a pointed rebuke for those who needed to turn from their abusive ways. They had become the proud without integrity, instead of the righteous who could live by faith (Hab. 2:4). We'll see the repeated pattern; their false worship had conformed them to make excuses for their own brutality.

While poetic justice would come for the Babylonians, it would also come for the "wicked" Habakkuk lamented in his first prayer (Hab. 1:4). The coming disaster should prompt them to reconsider their actions; this was their

2. See Genesis 18:19; Proverbs 31:8–9; Jeremiah 22:3.

call to repentance. It is ours as well. God calls us to see how we participate in injustice, to repent, and to walk by faith in lives transformed by Jesus.

The Mocking Song for Repentance

"Selfish thieves" or "greedy bullies" is probably not how we would describe ourselves, let alone "violent and cruel." Said another way, most of us assume we are not the targets of the woe song in Habakkuk 2. Still, the pictures painted should cause us to pause and consider.[3]

The lyrics condemn those who have used their power for their own gain. It's their power with money (v. 6), power to cheat (v. 9), power to harm (v. 12), and power to shame (v. 15) used to promote their status, ambitions, and ease, while pushing the cost on another. It's like a teeter-totter with one powerfully sliding the weights from his end, down the beam, and onto the other who sinks even further as a result—all because of the misuse of power.

Remember my Croatian apartment with the perilous balcony? We met the landlord after we agreed to rent it, a tall man in an expensive suit who was used to

---

3. Remember, poetry is designed to make us feel what others feel. We need help with empathy sometimes and the prophets are here for us, making us see and pay attention when we're distracted by whatever we want to do next. As you read the woe song again, take in the poetry as a warning against our own injustices.

fawning respect. He informed us immediately that he was a well-connected lawyer, allied to the local mob and former president. We'll call him Alen. We should be careful to keep in good relationship with him, Alen said. His bodyguard communicated the same message by his presence, as he was the largest man I'd ever met. Though his big scarce-toothed smile—covertly flashed at us—quieted fears, along with his appreciation for our homemade cookies. Alen was usually out of the country, as he worked at the Hague, he told us. It was later we learned, to our horror, that he defended those accused of war crimes in the Balkans.

Over the year we lived there, Alen would let himself into our apartment to "check on things." The irony that he always brought a bodyguard to march into an apartment of three twenty-something-year-old women was not lost on me. On one such occasion, our teenage friend was over visiting us, whom he propositioned before we could intervene.

When it comes to power in that country, I didn't know anyone with more. Alen had connections, money, prestige, and education. He had the financial, cultural, and positional power. And he leveraged all he had for protection and preservation of his lifestyle. Power kept him safe.

Whether we see it clearly or not, you and I have more power than we realize. We may not act like Alen, but the way we use our money impacts others. Our ability to maneuver circumstances filters into the well-being of our neighbors. Our words can shame with more force than we dare acknowledge. We protect our way of life, and sometimes we would do it even if it means pushing the cost to others.

Woe to Us?

Less than honorable use of power is easy in our culture, almost a norm; we're taught to leverage our resources to get where we want to go. The woe song urges us to acknowledge that how we swing the blade of power sets us up to clear the brambles on overgrown wilderness or to slice our neighbors. I'm with you on the journey to learn to live by faith rather than live using my power for my own self-protection.

We're going to return to the woe song of Habakkuk 2:6–20, this time with fresh eyes. As we take another look at these passages, we're going to read them not only as a denouncement of foreign oppressors outside of God's people, but also how the guilty parties *within Judah* would have heard it. The song cries out against those who misuse their power, and some of the wealthy amid God's own people would have seen themselves in the words. We may as well.

Financial Power

> "Woe to him who amasses what is not
>   his . . ."
> Woe to him who dishonestly makes
>   wealth for his house
> to place his nest on high,

**to escape the grasp of disaster!
(Hab. 2:6b, 9)**

Do you hear him call after the use of financial power in the first two stanzas? These words are not aimed solely at the Alens of the world, but to anyone who would harm others by only taking from them.

As business people, the integrity of how much you charge, how much you pay employees, and how many hours you require are addressed by Habakkuk and the rest of God's prophets. Whether it's the time of your people or the favor of coworkers, do you take and take with no intention of returning (v. 6)? Do you protect your "nest," knowing that refraining from generosity is law-breaking in the time of the prophets?

Our relationship with our own rights and own success has often clouded our view of God, for he cares much more for faithful living than excess profit made to pad our accounts.

This passage has destroyed my joy of bargain hunting. Well, most of it anyway. Sales and discount stores have been my go-to. To the great annoyance of my family, I'm slow to buy things if I think the price is too high, as I am sure I will find a better deal. (I see you, waiting-for-Black-Friday friends.) Yet, as you and I seek discounts, the cost goes somewhere. "Who is bearing the weight of it?" the prophets prompt us to ask. Perhaps a new technology has provided more affordable production, or a reorganization in distribution has lowered costs for the company. But in our worldwide economy, we must consider if we are pushing the burden from our side of the teeter-totter to the other because we are able, providing us a good deal and our global neighbors the load.

So, we ask: "Does the shirt I purchase at Target for very little mean that a family on the other side of the world is working in unhealthy conditions for unfair wages?"[4] It isn't visible to our eyes, but we often have power with our purchases to decide what those families are paid and what they endure. It's become the norm to find "good deals," even a Christian value cloaked in wise stewardship. Yet our society's desire for cheap fashion and new items impacts the vulnerable.

The ethics of the prophets push us toward kindness and integrity in our use of money. The compensation of the people who made the shirt on my back matters. The pay and treatment of those who do physical labor for my good matters. In my city, many of the manual labor teams for construction, harvesting, and yard work don't speak English, which impacts their ability to assure they are paid fairly. If we can get some cheap landscaping out of it, do we care? How often are we the selfish neighbors who take and take to make our lives easier, even if it costs the livelihood of other image-bearers?

My time spent in this section of Habakkuk's message has sent me on a journey for fair-trade purchases, used items, and keeping what we already own. It's

---

4. As I write, I believe that Target has experimented with a few fair-trade items, so check the tags.

harder this way. The question I keep asking myself is this: "Will we accept some cost to buy justly? Amid all our good desires to see other people use their power in benevolent ways, will *we* pay attention to the use of *our* power?"

Positional Power

> **Woe to him who builds a city with**
> **bloodshed**
> **and founds a town with injustice!** . . .
> **Woe to him who gives his neighbors**
> **drink,**
> **pouring out your wrath**
> **and even making them drunk,**
> **in order to look at their nakedness!**
> **(Hab. 2:12, 15)**

By way of reminder, the third stanza of Habakkuk's song speaks of those who would build a city on violence and injustice (v. 12). The fourth addresses the cruel use of shame to humiliate another for your own elevation (v. 15). It's the positional power the Babylonians have and the ferocity they'll use to do what they want.

If we look at the United States, we are not above unjust systems of positional power, so some gain and others are terrorized. Chattel slavery. Jim Crow laws. Theft of Native American land and genocide. While things have improved, the impact of such atrocities isn't gone, and neither is racism, on the small or large stage. It should humble us to use our power carefully, with input from others and open examination of the systems today. For example, we should notice if we want some people to make our cheap goods, but don't want them to live next door. Does that sound like using people as a commodity? We must also discern if we shame others because they point out misuse of positional power—it can feel tender and our pride would keep us from the effort it takes to change.

We're often oblivious to our own positional power within our greater culture, or within subcultures across our country. For instance, I take for granted the positive ways I am treated because of my family, ethnicity, language, and physical abilities. I have the ability to gain over others because of the preferences often given to me. What will we do with the cultural power before us? Our intense avoidance of suffering or loss of lifestyle can mean we look for shortcuts, the status quo, or non-conflict. Jesus told us following him was losing our lives (Matt. 16:25–26). The pursuit of comfort or ambition in efforts to "gain the world" bears only the fruit of greed and apathy.

Injustice often flows from our slowness to pay attention to how neighbors face the violence and shame from our society, and our repentance means centering more than our own experience. Jarvis Williams reminds us that if we live monoethnic lives, we're going to have monoethnic perspectives.[5] Another author calls for a

---

5. Dr. Williams is calling Southern Baptists specifically to change, but all can listen in and learn from him as well. Kevin

generation like Fannie Lou Hamer who won't back away from racist evils.[6] For some of us living in isolated, well-financed, white church bodies, we must enlarge our circles to include more black and brown believers from whom we can learn, in person and in books or podcasts. We must engage with those who have differing abilities and varying amounts of resources. Proximity matters, just as our passage speaks of attempts at isolation from those taken advantage of or neglected (hiding in a treetop nest, Hab. 2:9). In relationship, we hear about experiences of suffering and triumph, the sadness and joy, and remember to be slow to speak, quick to listen, and quick to lament. Our brothers and sisters help us see another perspective, changing our labeling of people as "other," but instead as those made in the likeness and image of God.[7]

We need gracious humility to learn, so that when a new law is announced or tragedy strikes, we can ask with some insight how it will impact our brother and sister who is a new immigrant, has a physical disability, or is in prison. The command to love one another isn't abstract but concrete—we use our cultural power

Jones and Jarvis J. Williams, *Removing the Stain of Racism from the Southern Baptist Convention: Diverse African American and White Perspectives* (Nashville: B&H Academic, 2017), 47.

6. Jemar Tisby, *How to Fight Racism: Courageous Christianity and the Journey Toward Racial Justice* (Grand Rapids: Zondervan, 2021), 44.

7. Albert J. Raboteau, "Forgiveness and the African American Church Experience," Transcript of an interview at the Faith Angle Forum, November 2015, 27–28.

to understand and care for others, rather than only ourselves.

Positional power includes so many categories. Bosses, parents, pastors, leaders, the nosy neighbor who seems to have the dirt on everyone—they have power. God's people use power for service, for protection of others, and for good, and any time it is used for unjust gain, Habakkuk's song would say, "Woe to you."

Warnings of Disaster that Lead Us to Repentance

God uses the warning of disaster to call for repentance against injustice.[8] So, reexamining the woe song, we ask the questions similar to those of my friends on 9/11. If the end is coming and God's judgment is here, will he also judge me for my ethics and use of power? My lifestyle, my attitudes, my purchases, my votes? Have they been to benefit me without considering how they impact other image-bearers?

Just like each call to repent from the prophets, the message required they turn from the pervading worldview. Habakkuk charged his hearers to see the powerplays and corruption of their fellow leaders for what they were—a sinking ship. The storm of judgment was on the horizon. While the party boat looked like everything was

8. In Nineveh, Jonah preached on the coming wrath of God and the Ninevites turned from their exploitative and violent behavior. Coming judgment pronounced brought revival and care for the harmed. Timothy Keller, *The Prodigal Prophet: Jonah and the Mystery of God's Mercy* (New York: Viking, 2018), 91.

fine, Habakkuk asked them to live like it was over and to trust God. This would look like inflating the lifeboats and jumping off a seemingly safe ship—crazy. Moving away from the "easy road" that harms others may look insane. Thinking that we sufferers are still called to care for those who are hurting will be dismissed by some. The church has been called crazy for this belief before; it will again as it chooses justice because of faith in a just God.

In December of 2018, Early Rain Covenant Church in Chengdu, China, a house church of hundreds of people, was brutally attacked. Half the congregation was detained, and many were beaten, including a grandmother in her seventies. All the church property, which filled a floor of an office building, was confiscated. The authorities did all they could to get the believers to leave the city. They forced landlords to end leases, glued front doors shut, and seized loved children many were fostering. The elders were arrested, and Pastor Wang Yi was sentenced to nine years of incarceration.[9] The persecution continues to this day.[10]

But what do our brothers and sisters say in their prayers when they are beaten down and raided again and again? They repent of their own injustice and apathy.

---

9. Read more about Pastor Wang Yi and his writings in Hannah Nation and J. D. Tseng, eds., *Faithful Disobedience: Wrightings on Church and State from a Chinese House Church Movement* (Downers Grove, IL: IVP Academic, 2022).

10. "Early Rain Covenant Church Urgent Prayer Updates," China Partnership, accessed December 8, 2021, https://www.china partnership.org/blog/2018/12/live-post-early-rain-covenant-church-urgent-prayer-updates.

Righteous Father, we repent to you for the Chinese house churches' inward focus in the midst of persecution. . . . Not only are we to live according to your holy law, but we are also to 'act justly and to love mercy and to walk humbly with your God.' Lord, we need to repent before you. In many things we have not witnessed your righteousness and have fallen short of your mercy: we have not prayed for the people of Hong Kong, we have not prayed for the people of Xinjiang, we have not even prayed for our brothers and sisters in bondage. . . . Lord, may your holy and good Spirit rebuke us, and your gracious Spirit uphold us, so that we may be strong and courageous, and remain faithful in the midst of persecution, not counting the gains and losses of this life, but thinking of the kingdom and the gospel of the last days, to testify and glorify your name![11]

These saints model to us what the Bible has already taught us—seeing hardship rightly urges us to repentance and lives of just action. They've faced worse than I ever have, and they repented of their apathy toward

---

11. Early Rain Covenant Church, "Merciful Heavenly Father: A Glimpse into the Weekly Prayer Life of Early Rain Covenant Church," China Partnership, January 6, 2022, https://www.chinapartnership.org/blog/2022/1/merciful-heavenly-father.

the Uyghur labor camps and genocide (referred to as the people of Xinjiang) and others in suffering and their own need to act justly. Another Chinese woman arrested for ministry says her humiliating and exhausting time in jail taught her to repent of her prejudice and anger.[12] For those of us facing hardship, the church in China models a soft heart and demonstrates how to use what power we have.

The life of faith is baffling to those on the outside. God's people choose a just orthopraxy inherent in our orthodoxy, even if our circumstances remain hard. Said another way, living by faith means right action always flows out of right belief.

When we are not faithful in how we use our power, Habakkuk's song points us to the root of the problem, addressed in the fifth and final stanza.

What Do You Worship?

What use is your false worship? the last stanza begins, pushing the warning "woe" to the second line, perhaps emphasizing the foolishness he's about to address. Here comes more "mocking" in the mocking song, because our trust in idols never makes sense.

**What use is a carved idol
after its craftsman carves it?**

---

12. Hannah Nation, "Building on Rock," Plough (blog), April 11, 2022, https://www.plough.com/en/topics/-community/church-community/building-on-rock.

> It is only a cast image, a teacher of lies.
> For the one who crafts its shape trusts
>   in it
> and makes worthless idols that cannot
>   speak.
> [19] Woe to him who says to wood: Wake
>   up!
> or to mute stone: Come alive!
> Can it teach?
> Look! It may be plated with gold and
>   silver,
> yet there is no breath in it at all.
> (Hab. 2:18–19)

The rhetorical questions are dripping with sarcasm. *Seriously, how can you think an idol you made is going to teach you? Still, ridiculously you tell the wood and stone to wake up!* Many of the rich people of Judah longed to be like the other nations and had adopted their gods, so these copycat idolators are stinging with the rebuke.

This topic may seem out of place compared to the arrogance, violence, and abuse we have seen so far in the song. But, if worship impacts our actions, then the core of this rebuke lands not only in the deeds but on the heart—their worship of an idol. Their morality wasn't rooted in the true living God, but in their own foolish pride and trust in self-directed religion.

Verse 19 asks "Can it teach?" and then answers its own question. Look—it's overlaid with gold and silver, but there's no breath in it, the lyrics say. Remember, it was the Lord God who breathed into the first people to give life (Gen. 2:7). That idol may be shiny and pretty, but it has no life to give, no spirit to speak. There's no way you're going to wake it up.

I grew up on a handful of green acres outside of a university town in Oregon. Our mini-ranch included a variety of animals, and within the family chore division, I was assigned the chickens for most of my years, along with plenty of stall-mucking and hay bale-bucking. Whenever I collected eggs from the chickens, I had to leave an egg in each nest to keep the chickens laying there. So as not to waste any, I would leave our ceramic eggs and carry all the fresh eggs into the house to wash. Sometimes a determined hen would sit on that ceramic egg all day like it was her own, convinced if she warmed it long enough it would hatch. But that clay egg was never going to wake. It would never come alive, and nothing she could do would make it otherwise. And so it was for the idol worshippers; they had no chance of instruction or life from those carved images.

When you worship what you made, you control what it says; your self-regulated worship leads to self-guided morality. Do you see yet how examining our worship will help us repent of our contribution to injustice?

While you and I may not be tempted to worship a piece of wood we carved and overlaid with silver, we worship things that we think will speak life to us. Those of us who worship fame will easily shame, lie, and neglect to gain more influence and followers. Or we adore certain "teachers" we watch on our phone, eating up ideologies that teach us to worship ourselves—*they tell me to do what feels best, so I will.* We use our power to satisfy our anxiety, discomfort, and disappointment, thus, we choose purchases that contribute to harm of global neighbors and policies to exclude those different than us.

Or we may idolize being on top. Our power is wielded to exclude those not "in" and manipulate with our decisions if opposed. Prizing security and money, we employ our financial power to horde or spend like we're building an empire. We worship our nets that bring us the richest of food, just like the Babylonians (Hab. 1:16).

We may not have carved an idol, but these are sculpted by our passions. They are for us, by us, and leading us toward apathy or perpetuating injustice. Idols center our desires on self. What is the idol sculpted by your desires? Fame, power, money, or even securing the perfect family life? What is it that is so valuable that it guides your morality?

Worshipping them is fruitless. For they will never speak to our souls. They will never wake up to help us. You can tend them as loyally as that settled hen, but they won't breathe life for you. If anything, idols will only pull you into greater evil and desperation.

But there is a God who speaks and whose Spirit breathes life. He has spoken from the beginning, his words creating the cosmos. His words bring life and truth—truth of his character, of his law, of his wisdom, and of his love. And like his speech at creation, he uses words to bring life to our souls. Ezekiel told the exiles that God would make dry bones live through the preaching of his message (Ezek. 37). The dead of us are brought spiritual life, that we know comes through the work of Jesus Christ.

The righteous live by faith in the words of this speaking God. We are not the proud who decide truth and justice for ourselves, like the arrogant in the beginning of Habakkuk 2:4. We belong to the Lord.

The end of the song brings all people to the end of themselves—the end of their own fantasy that an idol of their own making could rule as a god.

> **But the LORD is in his holy temple;**
> **let the whole earth**
> **be silent in his presence.**
> **(Hab. 2:20)**

The one who can speak—he demands silence and submission.

Those who have heard the words of the just God break their idols in repentance. It means it may cost more to do business or buy things ethically. It means we ask questions about the status quo in society, and we listen and do the work of repentance of our own prejudice and selfishness. It means our influence is used for service and not our ease. Our priorities realign. We use our power justly.

The God Who Stands against Injustice

The vision of the Lord in the holy temple also warns that Almighty, Holy God stands watching over those who are treated poorly.

In the jungle that is our neighborhood park, one day I watched our black three-year-old neighbor be told she couldn't play with a circle of children. A local kindergartner stood between the confused preschooler and a small group of kids and said they didn't play with girls with hair like hers. The racism was as obvious as the trees we stood under. Nannies and moms stepped in to correct, but the blonde kindergartner spokesman doubled down and declared her daddy was bigger than anyone, implying the not-present father would stand behind her and could legitimize her discrimination. The correction continued.

Still, a couple of us locked eyes in a knowing look. The blonde ringleader wasn't going to win her fight. Unknown to the kids, the father of the beautiful three-year-old was most definitely bigger than anyone's relation. He was a local NBA player, 6'8", and a man who lived by faith in Jesus Christ. As some might unjustly push this child aside and feel they have the power to do so, they don't realize who stands behind her. It's not just a tall, loving father—it is the Lord God King in his holy temple. He stands behind her, more powerful than any opposition, and he demands justice.

Our right use of power is motivated by our worship and our understanding of the God of justice we never want to oppose.

Repentance and Us

When I was living in Croatia, on a stormy afternoon I sat down to lunch with a local friend in a noisy cafeteria. I was about to ask her about her newly dyed purple hair, when it was clear she had something to say. She'd been watching the news and reading her history textbook. "Your people killed Native people. Your people stole and sold slaves. Your country still lives in racism to the point that it doesn't take care of black Americans! Your country dropped bombs over here, and our cancer rates rose because of it." I sat in shock and looked at her food, her, and my food while I tried to connect a thought. The pounding of the rain filled my ears.

I, of course, had read about those things, but I'd never had the responsibility for such crimes set at my feet. And after I took a breath, I realized I didn't want to be held responsible; I wanted to retaliate. After all, her country had been ruled by a communist regime that had murdered intellectuals, hunted religious leaders, and set up death camps. Corruption in the local religious systems meant the character of God was maligned. The bombs *our* country dropped ended the war against *her* people, in my view. But it didn't matter. Accusing her people of injustice didn't make my country less cul-pable for its own wrongdoing, and the circumstances were different. She and her family had suffered without power or control under every accusation of injustice I could think of. I, on the other hand, had been protected.

She was not wrong. My internal response was proud and ugly and digging for some way to avoid any semblance of guilt. I didn't personally make any of those decisions, but that wasn't her point. It was that there were consequences to evil done by people in my country. I was the only American she'd met, so I was present to hear about it. Her point was that my nation wasn't perfect, wasn't superior. Power had been used in evil ways. Again, she was not wrong.

We like to think of ourselves as those who have thought through justice and done things right, but if anything, our history should give us pause and make us suspicious when we're tempted to assert superiority to such things. There are corporate and individual injustices that have happened. So we pay attention and by faith are ready to repent—my apathy and actions have added to the unjust chaos of the world, even if I didn't make the decisions my purple-haired friend mentioned.

All of a sudden those targets of the woe song feel a bit closer to home. Who has been greedy, a bully, a mocker because of something we've wanted more than we've wanted to honor God? I'm raising my hand. I've valued my comfort and way of life at the expense of others, which includes ignoring racist practices. I've privileged those like me and declined to learn from others who are very wise. I've used power to belittle, make myself feel stable and important, and maintain a status quo that benefits me. I've purchased what saved me money but left others with not enough. It's my own actions and my own apathy from which I must repent.

The apathy toward harming another is a rejection of the command to love. Paul told the Roman church: "Let love be without hypocrisy. Detest evil; cling to what is good. Love one another deeply as brothers and sisters. Take the lead in honoring one another" (Rom. 12:9–10). He didn't change the subject mid-breath when he wrote "detest evil." He commands them to love sincerely, spelling it out for them. It means they must hate what is evil—as in evil actions against others. They are to love like siblings. The simile doesn't promote the brother who swipes his sister's lunch money, but the one who would protect her at all costs, even giving up his own greed or gain. It includes God's people paying attention to use of power.

Christ's Right Use of Power

"For even the Son of Man did not come to be served, but to serve, and to give his life as a ransom for many" (Mark 10:45). When we zoom out on the story of the incarnation, we realize that God the Son came into the creation he made for this purpose—to serve. He is the Son of Man, the One the Ancient of Days will exalt as king overall (Dan. 7:13–14). With all divine authority, he chose to take the form of a human to be a servant, humbling himself (Phil. 2:6–8). The greatest person to ever live used his power to serve.

His perfect law-keeping and his perfect character show us the recapitulation of every failed human. He did it right. We have failed. He loved those he could have ostracized. He welcomed and gave to those in need. He never gained from the loss of another. His ethics showed what image-bearing should be.

We may have never literally invaded and plundered, but we have taken what was not ours. We have sought to protect ourselves while taking advantage of others (Hab. 2:9). We have worshipped things that cannot teach us the truth and have no life in themselves to give (Hab. 2:18–19). We are to live justly in all things, but we have not and cannot. But Jesus did (Isa. 42:1–4).

Because of his full life of justice, you and I can be justified. God is just and the justifier because of Jesus's perfect life and death (Rom. 3:26). So, if we believe the gospel, we can be honest about our failure. *We can repent.*

Oppression makes life easier, and it will cost us to fight it. But it is a fight worth everything. It is the way of Jesus, who used his power to serve, receiving harm and upending the oppression of sin. His transforming power leads us into just lives.

So one day we will be able to stand in that throne room without the woes coming onto our heads. We will instead worship, justified. Today we repent of our idols. Today we choose to live by faith with just interactions—for one day we will see the glory of the Lord. It's the glory that is even now flooding the earth and giving us hope.

Chapter 6

Faith in the Glorious King

God: "Knowledge of my glory will fill the earth."

"When one bases his senses on the glory of the coming world that no ear has heard, no eye has seen, and no mind has conceived, it is impossible not to rejoice. You have felt and tasted of the coming glory—even though the circumstances you are going through are still difficult."

—Noah Wang, Chinese house church pastor[1]

Strangers eyed marks on my arms and legs for eight years during my twenties and thirties. The usually small bruises weren't painful, just obvious. I'd have two on a leg and another on an arm almost constantly. The reoccurring bruises showed up for two reasons: first, because I'm naturally clumsy. It's true. Second, because

---

1. Noah Wang, "Test of Faith," in *Faith in the Wilderness: Words of Exhortation from the Chinese Church*, ed. Hannah Nation and Simon Liu (Bellingham, WA: Kirkdale Press, 2022), 119.

I was also on a medication that came with a side effect of easy bruising.

The purple or blue bruises were brought up often. People at work, friends, and even strangers in a parking lot pointed out the discolorations. These were usually warm encounters and an expression of concern, when I would respond with surprise as I forgot I looked injured. I would try to assure them that I was just a woman with thinned blood who runs into things.

The comments revealed something real about our perception of the world. They suspected wrongdoing when they saw a young woman speckled with bruises, and normally, they wouldn't be wrong in doing so. One woman I met in a shop slipped me a domestic violence pamphlet. I restrained my desire to bear-hug her for her courageous care for a stranger. Even though I assured her I slipped on a wet floor to get the bruise she saw, she didn't believe me.

She was too suspicious of abuse and manipulation. I don't blame her (though I really did slip on a wet floor). Cynicism feels like the natural outcome of living in this broken and corrupt world, and sometimes the outcome of reading the biblical prophets, if we're honest. So where's the hope when we desperately want good? If God judges, then what? Where is this all going?

Habakkuk has been seeking those answers. The Lord told Habakkuk that judgment was coming for Judah, and coming in the form of the Babylonians. Habakkuk's stomach lurched as ours would have, and he offered a prayer of protest. How could this be right if the invaders were worse than the people of Judah? Habakkuk stood waiting to hear from the Lord with gritty faith and was given a vision for how he and the people could continue on—by that same faith, even if they trembled. The Lord's righteous ones will live by faith in him as their faithful and just God. They live by faith, looking ahead to his work to come in the midst of chaos.

The Lord didn't stop there; he went on to give the people a mocking song. It's the song we've been reading for the last two chapters, and we will spend a little more time in it because there are still more questions to explore. We've acknowledged that our just God is going to bring judgment, but it is still hard to understand how the evil of the world and its consequences offer real hope. How does this fit into a good plan of God? Are we headed to something better?

Many years ago, I was traveling and found myself lost. Not just the "it's going to take a bit longer" kind of lost, but the kind that sounds like "what am I going to do?" I had been studying at a foreign university in Western Europe and had taken a train to the big city nearby. This was before smartphones. Do you remember traveling back then? In case you don't, let me tell you that being lost and alone without GPS, data, or an app with a map felt a bit different. After taking my second bus that someone had recommended, I finally found the paper map wadded up in the bottom of my backpack. I'd already asked three people for help in a language that I was still learning and was considering giving up. That meant a long walk back to a bus I hoped was going the direction of my hostel (no ride-share apps, remember?). I came to the rise of another hill with lagging dedication to my adventure when I found a landmark, then a street name that matched the map. I knew where I was and where I was going.

There is a fog that comes from grief that can feel a lot like being lost. We have been staring at abuse, by our hands or hands of others, and it's understandably exhausting and disorienting. We need a map that shows us where we are, the landmarks of God's plan, and the destination to which God will surely deliver us. He's the just God who judges, but that's not the ultimate end.

Friend, this song points us to what is.

The Earth Will Be Filled

Whenever my husband and I hug our daughter in a group hug, she throws her hands in the air and yells, "I'm the jelly!" Her favorite part of a PB&J lunch is the jelly, and she's sure that our arms wrapped around her are a sandwich. Sometimes when we read a Bible passage, the content is enveloped, forming layers and giving emphasis to something in the middle—like the jelly. (Though I'm sure some of you are going to argue with me that the MVP is the peanut butter, and I won't quibble.) There's some jelly for us in this passage.

If we remember the middle of the song that we looked at in previous chapters, we'll recall that the third stanza goes like this:

> **Woe to him who builds a city with**
> **bloodshed**
> **and founds a town with injustice!**
> **Is it not from the Lord of Armies**
> **that the peoples labor only to fuel the**
> **fire**
> **and countries exhaust themselves for**
> **nothing?**
> **For the earth will be filled**
> **with the knowledge of the Lord's glory,**
> **as the water covers the sea.**
> **(Hab. 2:12–14)**

It's the woe against the violent, those who gain from oppression. It tells us what happens to everyone who tries such a life—they get exhausted futility. Woe to them! The Lord knows how to make them work only to watch it all burn to nothing.

But the Lord's work is not like theirs. It is much greater than theirs and it does not burn. His work will last, and it will fill the earth. The knowledge of the Lord's glory will inundate like the water in the sea. *This, my friend, is the jelly—the big picture and the hope of what God is doing.*

It feels a bit strange to come to a place of talking about the knowledge of God's glory spreading in the midst of pronounced punitive measures. But even as God is using this song to comfort the suffering with coming justice, he also wants us to know that he is working on mission to bring the world to a place of grasping his glory.

From the very beginning of Israel's history, God declared his intention for all the world to know him.[2] Remember the miraculous works against Pharoah to free his people, so that all would know who he is (Exod. 9:14, 16, 29)? Remember the prophetic messages that have pointed to the consequences coming on wicked nations and the future welcoming them into the people of God (Isa. 2:2–5; 49:6)? Even in his condemnation of evil, God is working his plan to reveal himself.

So the mission of God has not been forgotten in this discussion of his justice. Smack in the middle of the song of poetic reversals of cruelty is a declaration that the earth will not be filled with the evil of men but with the knowledge of the glory of the Lord. It's as if God is telling them their wicked work will fail *because* God's work won't. God is bringing the knowledge of his glory to the entire world.

Knowledge is a relational term in Hebrew. This is not knowledge that would fill a textbook, but knowledge that would fill a personal note. Like the way you write a note to your patient and loving parent on their birthday. You know them in a way that the words you say hold a lot more meaning to your designated reader than they

2. Kenneth L. Barker and Waylon Bailey, *Micah, Nahum, Habakkuk, Zephaniah: An Exegetical and Theological Exposition of Holy Scripture,* New American Commentary (Nashville: Holman Reference, 1998), 340.

would to a stranger who found the note years later. You grasp who they are and show it in how you write.

The knowing of God's glory is coming, as promised, not from universal seminary study, but because he will make every mind grasp what he's like, what he has done, and how great he is. His glory will be unmissable, something we can know through experience.

Glory can be an obtuse word. It most often springs from our lips in Christmas carols, but even then we typically tie it to the singing of shiny angels. Glory is God's brilliant beauty that we see in his character and action. It's his grace, his loveliness. It is also his holiness and righteousness that reveal him as utterly unique and worthy, when we are not. It means he deserves the praise, the honor, for he is the glorious King.

The man in 36A sat next to me as we flew the length of California. I had just swapped seats mid-flight with my husband, so he could take his turn to wrangle our small, energetic child. I said hello to my new seatmate, and we started talking. I found out he had studied philosophy for nine years, teaching it in university and then leaving it for a career in technology. He began to speak about purpose, and our conversation turned to the purpose of life. (I love conversations on airplanes.) He described his master's thesis on the purpose of living, gaining insight from the purpose of inanimate objects in the world. I offered an idea from the Westminster Shorter Catechism, that our purpose is tied to giving glory to God, our Creator. Setting aside the controversial idea of a Creator for a few minutes, we tried to dissect the word *glory*. It wasn't easy.

Understandably, he had a hard time seeing "glory" as a positive word. One thinks of fame-seeking or superiority, perhaps even a violent victory. I attempted to describe the meaning of the Hebrew word for glory. Giving glory is to show how great God is. Glory is richness, abundance, and splendor. He looked at me like I was nuts. I tried again: "It's a weight of excellence, praise, and honor." His brow still wrinkled. He asked a few questions about etymology that didn't help much. He and I had each studied a handful of languages, but the only overlapping one was English. Finally, he suggested that it would make sense if we used the word *glorious*. His secular perspective could acknowledge sometimes circumstances were glorious—good and awe-inducing. He could even envision how this world was *supposed* to reflect something glorious.

What are things that you've seen as *glorious*? One friend recently used the word when he saw a feast served for the large gathering. While that may seem a lightweight use of the term, I felt his point. It was excellent and beautiful, overwhelmingly better than expected or deserved. Perhaps you've felt the word watching a sunset or standing at the viewpoint after a good hike. God's glory is even better—in perfection and worth. It humbles us and puts us in awe.

Habakkuk says that "the earth will be filled with the knowledge of the LORD's glory, as the water covers the sea" (Hab. 2:14), and he's not the first one to say so.

It's a theme through the Scriptures, as we'll find out. Habakkuk is pointing along with others to what God is doing and where we're going.

The coming of the knowledge of God's glory offers hope like a flood in the desert of injustice. Our trajectory to that end means God doesn't leave evil to win; he will bring justice. It means God doesn't leave us alone; his presence is promised for us. It means God doesn't leave us to fix this world ourselves; he has revealed his glory to save us. This is the hope of his people and the final destination on the map—the glory of God for all to see.

Not Scorched without His Justice

I grew up in a family always looking for ways to be in the water, which my husband reminds me isn't the common experience. As kids, we'd visit a cabin on the Oregon coast. My sister and I would drag the beat-up tandem kayak out from beside the cabin, tell our black retriever to jump in the back, and paddle down the river to where the bay converged into the Pacific Ocean. We'd have to carry the plastic kayak over the sand when the flow turned ankle-deep and rocky. Then we'd push it through the waves, looking for seals to feed, giving them some of the scallops we'd snatched from the freezer. Sometimes the kayak swerved parallel to the waves, and the water would grab the boat edge and pull it down like a lever, flipping us into the saltwater. We'd tumble under the surface for a bit and pop back up, looking for the boat. Back in we climbed, grabbing the faithful dog by his collar to pull him in too. After we evaluated what we lost when we capsized, usually just the frozen seal-snacks, we'd surf the next wave back to the beach, laughing and wet.

When we read "the earth will be filled with the knowledge of the LORD's glory, as the water covers the sea" (Hab. 2:14), the imagery paints a picture of the greatness of the ocean. We couldn't imagine a "sea" without water covering over land, and so it is with the coming knowledge of God's glory. It will be so enveloping, it will flood every last inch.

And for some, thinking about getting thrown around in the ocean sounds wonderful, like my childhood memories in a shallow bay and the smell of our wet dog. But now that I'm older, getting rolled under the water by freezing, hard-to-predict waves doesn't sound like entertainment. The dangers of the undertow and power of the surge feel more ominous as I know what they can do. The coming revelation of God's glory isn't purely child's play. I've read respected teachers who quote this verse out of context, making it anemic by ignoring the woes against injustice in which it falls. His glory comes from a true Judge who deals with evil.

The Lord's glory is shown when he holds righteous standards as a holy God in keeping with his character, and it's shown when he brings justice against those who fail to keep those standards. Just judgment is part of revealing the glory of our God.

God has been talking about his glory filling the world for a long time and tied it to his dealing with wrongdoing and lack of faithfulness (Num. 14:21). So, here in an onslaught of woes, God promises his glory is going to be revealed. In this passage, the whole message of the twelve minor prophets hangs in the balance. Judgment is being poured out, the nations fall exhausted, the prophets bow in awe, and Yahweh reigns with his coming glory.[3] His plan is pushed forward by his character as a righteous God giving just consequences to purify Judah and judge their enemies.

This is solace for us in the chaos. He doesn't leave us scorched from the fire of injustice. God will deal with the evil, not only because he is just, but also because it is on his path to spreading his glory throughout the earth. Nothing is going to stop his plan of redemption for the world.

We see hints of this today, like the light peeking through the dark curtains when you're ready for daybreak. It's when those in power bring right consequences on those who abused and oppressed. It's when people acknowledge the wrong and act to restore. Sometimes we see justice happening, and it tastes of the beauty and splendor of God.

His glory is shown when he judges *and* when he exhibits his love and faithfulness in bringing salvation for his people, first in the return from exile and then in a salvation that results in his glory stretching around the

---

3. Paul R. House, *The Unity of the Twelve*, The Library of Hebrew Bible/Old Testament Studies (Sheffield, England: Sheffield Academic Press, 2009), 147.

world, emanating from Jerusalem.[4] Judgment isn't the only step on the path to revealing God's glory. God's glorious salvation is going to bring his inundating presence.

Not Parched without His Presence

My friend in 36A moved on from our discussion on the purpose of life and shared about the big changes for he and his girlfriend. Recently, they had spent nine months in Hawaii. One of his favorite things was when his roommate took them out into the ocean to swim with a pod of seventy spinner dolphins. Surrounding the handful of people, the dolphins were curious and playful, interacting with each other as they examined the swimmers. He struggled to describe the feeling of being in their presence. I asked if it was glorious. He laughed and agreed. Breathtaking. Indescribable.

If that is what the presence of a pod of dolphins evokes in us, imagine what the glorious presence of God will do when it is fully unleashed across the world. We've talked about God's glory as his character, but it's also his active presence, tied specifically to his name and choice to be with his covenant people (Exod. 33:18–19). It's awe-inspiring, holy, and scary for lawbreakers like us. Yet this is what we are longing for—God's full presence. You know what that feeling is? When you watch the Spirit of

---

4. James M. Hamilton Jr., *God's Glory in Salvation through Judgment: A Biblical Theology* (Wheaton, IL: Crossway, 2010), 233–34.

God speak through his Word, in the quiet of your home or the gathering of his people. When you sing to him and want to never stop, or even when grief makes you yearn for his comfort—you want more of him. We want to know him and experience him, the great King for whom our hearts were made.

In multiple places in the Bible, the filling with glory is associated with God's manifest presence filling the tabernacle, and then his temple, as the people looked on with awe and gratitude. Just imagine watching God come to dwell with you as you travel in the wilderness (Exod. 40:33–38). Breath taken away, you stand and hear the priestly blessing after seeing God's glory rush upon his finished tent.

> "May the LORD bless you and protect you;
> may the LORD make his face shine on you
> and be gracious to you;
> may the LORD look with favor on you
> and give you peace."
> (Num. 6:24–26)

You've just seen it in the glory consuming the tabernacle. And through tears you realize the visible presence of God is his blessing for you. From there in his presence, he will shine on you. From there, he will give you favor. From there, he will give you peace.[5]

---

5. Greg Beale shows how this blessing was likely first pronounced on the day that Moses finished setting up the tabernacle and the blessing was likely God's glorious presence they'd just seen come upon the tabernacle. G. K. Beale, *The Temple and*

Isn't that what we most deeply want? *God, bring your glory and your presence in my life,* we pray. Now, the Israelites looked to his presence in the tabernacle (and later in the temple) for their worship and God's steadfast love. It was there that God dwelled. But they couldn't really enter his presence. Only the high priest once a year entered the Holy of Holies, for God's glorious presence excluded sin.

Thus, knowing God's glorious presence also makes us realize who we are, like when Isaiah saw the throne room of God in his heavenly temple (Isa. 6:1–5). The heavenly beings hovered, calling out God's holiness and how his glory filled the earth. What did Isaiah do? He recognized his sin. He called down woe upon himself, just like the woes of Habakkuk's song, for the prophet knew he wasn't good and right. God's glory exposes sin. And in the pattern of our gracious God, Isaiah's sin was atoned for, and Isaiah could be in the heavenly temple with the glorious King (vv. 6–7). There's a tension in wanting God's glory as we desire his presence but also knowing our sin cannot stand before him. We need the atonement Isaiah received.

God revealed the goodness of being in his glorious presence. He poured out his glory to dwell in a structure on earth and even lifted Isaiah to see him in the heavens, but now he is doing more. His promise here isn't just about his glory in the temple in Jerusalem, but Habakkuk

---

the *Church's Mission: A Biblical Theology of the Dwelling Place of God* (Downers Grove, IL: IVP Academic, 2004), 402.

records of his splendor reaching across the globe with his presence to fill everywhere. No place will be parched for lacking the glorious knowledge of God.

The God Who Brought Justice and Glory

When you encounter something glorious and weighty, it shakes you. Like dropping a heavy boot into a puddle, it displaces the water and sends it in a spray. Andrew Wilson describes it: "The weightier substance displaces the flimsy one, and the flimsy one shakes, gives way, and is forced to reorient itself around the weight of glory."[6] Isaiah had been shaken.

Isaiah saw the Lord in his throne room, recognized God's glory, and was changed. He later wrote about a person who would fill the earth with the knowledge of the Lord *as the waters cover the sea.* The destination of the world was a glory-filled earth because of the coming Spirit-anointed one from David's family—the coming Messianic King!

Does that person reflect the themes of God's glory we've talked about so far? The coming of the promised King involves consequences for evil and justice; it's a King who knows how to care for people with right judgments, like the divine King speaking to Habakkuk. His righteousness and faithfulness will lead to joy, security,

6. Andrew Wilson, *God of All Things: Rediscovering the Sacred in an Everyday World*, Illustrated edition (Grand Rapids: Zondervan, 2021), 18.

and peace because of the knowledge of God spread like the sea (Isa. 11:6–9).

There was a person coming who would reveal God's glory, and Habakkuk knew it from reading what Isaiah wrote one hundred years earlier. Here Habakkuk records in his song from the Lord a reminder that the knowledge of God's glory would fill the whole earth, and he knew the Lord would do it through the Messiah who would be Judge and Savior. He would overthrow the kingdom of the world to get us to a place of final peace and joy.

And that is what happened. The glory of the Lord came to earth outside the temple, in the Spirit-filled incarnate Son of God. When the Word became flesh, he dwelt among us and revealed his glory (John 1:14).

But Jesus's life feels like the opposite of what our woe song sings. Shame should fall on those who oppose Jesus. He shouldn't be shunned and left in poverty. He shouldn't experience trickery and violence. Where are the promised consequences against the wicked in the life of the One bringing God's glory?

See, in a reversal unexpected by our ease and success-loving perspective, glory came through Jesus walking through the violence and suffering described in the woes.

Jesus accomplished his mission in the most unforeseen way—he died on a cross, an instrument of shame and humiliation, and said that it was his way to glory (John 12:23). His glory cannot be separated from the cross; rather his humiliating death reveals the glorious character of God.[7] A God who rescues by carrying the entire load of covenantal punishment, who wins justice through humility, sacrificial love, and vicarious judgment. As John Calvin said, "For in the cross of Christ, as in a magnificent theatre, the inestimable goodness of God is displayed before the whole world."[8] The cross revealed God's glorious plan; it's the landmark indicating the road leading to the journey's end—"this is the road to God's glory filling the earth."

Do you see it? From this view, can you see where we're going?

Jesus dealt with evil and injustice by conquering the enemy and securing the final judgment that will fall. And through his death and resurrection, we have the presence of God breaking out of the temple, with a torn curtain for evidence (Matt. 27:51). In the Spirit, God comes ablaze on his people, now defined by their faith in the glorious King who lived, died, and rose again in their place.

It's the rushing flow of the knowledge of the glory of God to meet us in the arid desert of chaos and the heartbreaking abuse of power. Our own unbearable shame has been cleansed and our need for justice has been secured. You now know foretastes of the complete glorious presence of God in his Spirit, who is whispering

---

7. Jeremy R. Treat, *The Crucified King: Atonement and Kingdom in Biblical and Systematic Theology* (Grand Rapids: Zondervan, 2014), 161.

8. John Calvin, *Commentary on the Gospel According to John. A New Translation, from the Original Latin, Volume Second*, trans. William Pringle, vol. 2 (Amsterdam: Leopold Classic Library, 2010), 73.

to your heart that the Lord loves you like a good father, even when you hurt (Rom. 8:15).

Streams Waiting for the Flood

Our family (on the mini-ranch) lived down a long gravel lane in what was called Soap Creek Valley. Beside the country road were ditches that flowed as streams almost year-round, fed by Oregon's rain and a few springs. Culverts ran under the road whenever needed, directing the water under driveways and off-shoot streets. But when the rain was fierce and those culverts plugged, the water would flood, surging over the only road in and out of the valley. It's current poured under fences, around warning signs, and through fields, neglecting boundaries and property lines. You don't contain water at that point. It was going to spread across the low points of the entire valley, and you just wait.

Knowledge of the glory of the gospel is like that water; it's going to spread. Some of the final words written in the book of Isaiah say the Lord will send some of his people "to the nations . . . who have not heard about me or seen my glory. And they will proclaim my glory among the nations" (Isa. 66:19). Now we, the people of the King, speak to the world of the glorious gospel of Jesus. It's as if the power of the first light at creation exploded in our hearts when we saw God's glory in Jesus Christ. We're forever changed, tasting the new creation begun in us. So, we are servants who cannot give up speaking, for God has shown us his glory (2 Cor. 4:1–6). Nothing will stop the spread.

We're the streams dispersing across the world, irrigating the harvest field as the Spirit of God brings that light of the knowledge of God's glory in the face of Jesus to new hearts. We're the new temple, built from people of all ethnicities, so filled with his glorious presence that we manifest it to those around us.[9] We labor, but we know we don't fix this world ourselves. We're the streams waiting for the flood.

Yet, even as we wait, we still long for the knowledge of God to be experiential, like it is holding the hand of a loved one as you walk down the road rather than another video call with a screen between you. So we, too, get tastes of intimacy with God, as we read, pray, sing, and experience the fellowship of his Spirit. But it makes us long for something more—a fuller presence of God. The glorious presence that also encompasses every nook and cranny of the broken world to make things right.

My husband and I once went looking for dolphins, like my airplane seatmate had. We imagined exactly what he described, an incomparable experience, being surrounded by these large, social marine mammals. We paid for a "guaranteed" swim with a wild pod and climbed onto the boat. Ultimately, we left having seen no dolphins but having endured hours of seasickness.

Sometimes we're looking for expressions of God's glory filling the earth—his justice breaking through,

---

9. Beale, *The Temple and the Church's Mission*, 402.

his people living in sacrifice and love, a new grasp of his glory—and instead we find the revolting twisting of goodness and ourselves hanging over the side of a boat losing our lunch. As we face injustice that still lives on the earth, we're reminded that we've not yet made it to a world inundated with the knowledge of his glory.

Our brothers and sisters who were enslaved in the United States knew what it meant to face injustice while believing in God's glory to come. Their historic spirituals testify to a paradoxical combination of suffering and hope.[10] The choruses call out for the spiritual deliverance brought in Christ and the just physical freedom the enslaved sought. It was through gospel joy that they spoke of the future, one of glory and of coming judgment. Albert Raboteau points to their example in human suffering and asserted trust in God, even as their faith is expressed as "Nobody knows de trouble I see. Nobody knows but Jesus. Nobody knows de trouble I've had. Glory hallelu."[11]

So we await the new creation, like our brothers and sisters have from the time of the Fall, looking forward to when the glorious presence of God will truly fill the entire earth. Then the whole earth will stand before King Jesus who will judge the living and the dead in justice and righteousness (Rev. 19–20), and the dwelling of God will be with us (Rev. 21–22). The glory of the Lord will no longer

---

10. Albert J. Raboteau, *Slave Religion: The "Invisible Institution" in the Antebellum South*, updated edition (Oxford; New York: Oxford University Press, 2004), 243–66.

11. Raboteau, *Slave Religion*, 258–59.

radiate from a temple, but instead from the Lamb himself whose light is enough for all. In the light of his glory, we'll dwell, for the knowledge of the Lord's glory will fill the earth as the water covers the sea. Glory hallelu.

Faith in the Glorious King

There's a map that shows us where we're going. We're not stuck on a terrifying carousel of ups and downs, just waiting for when the woes will come. We see the endgame—a flood of the knowledge of God's glory.

For now, we often wait in lament, asking: "How long, Lord?" and "When will we see your righteous justice permeate all that we see?" When the persecution of brothers and sisters rises in places and there is little we can do but pray, we know God's glory is coming. When the powerful overrun the unprotected, and we fear a broken system will not hold anyone accountable, we know God's glory is coming. We know, we will see it, even if we advocate, speak, act, and pray today with little impact next week. The earth will be flooded one day with the good knowledge of God's glory. Good in all the senses—justice, righteousness, and holiness.

That's why we can begin our laments loud and end them in trusting silence before the glorious King in his heavenly temple, just like the end of this woe song prescribes. It's a holy hushing that declares final justice comes by the hand of God and not human action. We lay down our own strategies to rule this world and turn from our own glory-seeking. The hushed pause embraces faith in God's future filling of the earth with his glory and stands on the truth that God has already revealed justice in Jesus Christ. This is the big picture, the glimpse from the heights, for you and for me. And for the whole world.

"God never abandoned the purpose of causing his glory to cover the land as the waters cover the sea."[12] And he never will.

12. Hamilton, *God's Glory in Salvation through Judgment*, 51.

Section 3

WAITING AND JOY

Chapter 7

Faith in the God Who Rescues

"God, do it again."

*"And thus it is written, 'The just lives by faith,' for we do
not as yet see our good, and must therefore live by faith;
neither have we in ourselves power to live rightly, but
can do so only if He who has given us faith to believe
in His help do help us when we believe and pray."*

—Augustine, fourth-century bishop of Hippo in North Africa[1]

After a couple months of training (because we're not the most athletic bunch), my sister and I were ready for our backpacking trip. We'd been planning it for almost a year—going into the high desert wilderness known for its beauty. After starting out, we came to a bridge over a ravine and creek. We paused to discuss

---

1. Augustine of Hippo, "The City of God," in *St. Augustine's City of God and Christian Doctrine*, ed. Philip Schaff, trans. Marcus Dods, vol. 2, A Select Library of the Nicene and Post-Nicene Fathers of the Christian Church, First Series (Buffalo, NY: Christian Literature Company, 1887), 401.

our next move, perhaps because the "bridge" was really a few long, unsecured boards. Our questions bounced back and forth, intensified by the fact that neither of us knew the trail. "Is it strong enough?" The boards swayed a bit as you stepped onto them, and we had thirty-five-pound packs on our backs. Yet it seemed to be well used, so we supposed it sturdy. "Wait, is this the direction we need?" In the dearth of plants in the high desert, the sandy soil stretches from tree to tree with a handful of bushes and sagebrush. It's hard to recognize the trail. It was possible that we'd wandered to a new path. How did we know if it would even help us get to our destination?

Our questions of the makeshift bridge are often what we ask of God when we've come to an impasse. In our waiting for justice, is he strong enough to help? And will he do what we need? Is he even the kind of God to take us where we need to be? we speculate. Ultimately, we're asking: "Is God able to help?" and "Is God willing to help?"

Our questions push us back to what we know about God. Habakkuk's been on this same journey with the Lord, wrestling with evil he sees around him and how God could use evil people as his instruments of judgment. He's heard an answer from the Lord. It describes the judgment of the proud and the way to survive—the righteous shall live by their faith (Hab. 2:4). Live by faith watching for God to bring justice.

We get to the last chapter of the book, and it's as if Habakkuk has been mulling on what he heard. You know when you get the news you didn't expect and didn't really want, you have to process it. For me, that would mean I'm talking about it left and right, and my husband would have heard thousands of words angling it from every direction. If *he* heard hard news, he would say very little but would be pondering his response. The sorting of emotions, analysis of worldview, and calculating a reaction is done completely inside his mind—which is still baffling to this verbal processor.

Whichever way Habakkuk processed, he was doing it. He wanted his next words to lead—to be words that pointed to the God who rescues and to the way to survive.

A Hymn to the Heart

If we remember the emotional context of Habakkuk, we recall that God's people were anxious and afraid (not unlike our struggles today). The leadership and privileged of the population were corrupt, and God had said the long-predicted exile was coming. God was going to judge his people. Yet he'd also given them the five woes against the violent and arrogant abusers to reassure of justice. The woes culminate in a vision of the Lord God in his temple and the earth keeping silent before him. His power, sovereignty, holiness, and place as judge shine through. Justice would come against the wicked of Judah and against their evil invaders in due time.

So what does living by faith look like as they wait? What does it look like for us if we wait for justice as we strive to trust the Lord? That's exactly what Habakkuk shows us. The word *faith* isn't in the final chapter of this book, but the entire passage fleshes out how it's done. Habakkuk is going to live out the call of God that the righteous live by faith—in poetry.

You would guess Habakkuk had been meditating on the Psalms, because he writes a hymn for them to sing (Hab. 3:1). Some have argued that Habakkuk was a Levite, working in the temple and, thus, explaining his tendency to write for the community worship. We don't know if he was a temple worker or not, but this psalm was written for God's people to sing together and to soothe their hearts.

It's as if the prophet knew the people didn't need a sermon when they ached from grief and trembled with fear. They needed words put into their mouths for a song. The lyrics would answer their questions, remind, and meet their distrust.

I'm guessing I'm not the only one who has belted out what I was feeling with no audience to hear. Our car dashboards could tattle of our tears to heartbreaking ballads, the shouts with angry lyrics, and the worship songs that turned us to repentance when we needed it. The words of songs infiltrate our souls. God knows when we need this; so does Habakkuk.

The Prayer

What do you think of when you hear the name Bill Clinton? Or when you hear the name Billy Graham?

Or Joseph Stalin? Or Pope Francis? All are people with immense power whose actions have been recorded in thousands of pages. Now imagine that you were going to have a conversation with one of them. You'd be gathering in your mind all that you'd heard about what they'd done. You'd be on your way to the conversation, remembering all the reports which have given you a picture of who they are and what they are like, right?

And so, Habakkuk reminds us to gather in our minds the works of the Lord, as he launches his psalm. He begins with a one-verse prayer:

> **Lord, I have heard the report about**
> **you;**
> **Lord, I stand in awe of your deeds.**
> **Revive your work in these years;**
> **make it known in these years.**
> **In your wrath remember mercy!**
> **(Hab. 3:2)**

Do you hear him? He says, *Lord, I've heard about you. I know what you do.* Like the fame of past political and religious leaders, Habakkuk knows the report about God. But his record is different than any other, for it is not filled with mixed reports of heroism and scandal. It does not hold evidence of both wise leadership and compromise. It does not tell a tale of advocating for your people in one moment and then turning your back on them the next.

It's the Lord's curriculum vitae slid across a desk at an interview—he is the covenant God, a God who has bound himself to his people. His past works speak to his character and his ability. It's not just intellectual comprehension of his deeds; the opening words say that they produce awe. The rest of the song will lay them out for us.

We're going to remember his constancy, his goodness, and his action. He's the God who has shown up when we were desperate. In remembering, we say, "Lord, do it again." "Revive your work" is how Habakkuk phrases it (v. 2). *Lord, you've said that the righteous will live by faith, so make us live.*

Like when you're in that middle school play and you look to your fellow performer, only to find him on stage next to you frozen, dazed by the lights and staring into the audience. Through your nodding, you're trying to communicate: "Now! Now's the time. Say your line! Do the thing I know you know how to do."

Revive your work, Lord. You've acted before, now do it again.

Next, the prayer asks God to do it where Habakkuk can see. "Make it known in these years," Habakkuk writes (v. 2). He doesn't just want the Lord to work, he also wants his people to see it *in these times*. Don't do it through your behind-the-scenes handiwork but bring a dazzling delivery for the fearful to see. May those living by faith see you make them stand.

There are times when we as God's people may feel like those huddled in the corner, begging God to do something. Facing hardship like those before us, we pray for our God to rescue us, and we pray for encouragement for our brothers and sisters, that they may watch it happen.

Recently, Middle Eastern pastors have told stories of religious extremists visiting their churches with nefarious intent only to have their minds changed.[2] God's people watched those who wanted to hurt them return with respect, and some even come to faith in the true King. Secular academics who study extremism are looking for answers and are now reading about the deradicalization done by these churches. Not that deradicalization was the goal of the church, but the change from militant, radical Muslim to one open to working with other faiths came as a by-product of their mercy ministry, gospel message, and offering themselves as a family with open arms. *Help us to see your work, Lord; do more of this. So much so that secular academics want to study the change from violence to respect. Do it again and in our cities as we see brokenness and devised violence.*

Habakkuk closes his prayer pleading with God to remember mercy. They are going into exile, after all. *Mercy* here is a word related to how God defined himself to Moses, translated there as compassionate (Exod. 34:6). *You are a compassionate God, so operate by your compassion for us, even as you judge, Lord.*

---

2. Jayson Casper, "The Secret to Deradicalizing Militants Might Be Found in Middle Eastern Churches," ChristianityToday.com, November 22, 2021, https://www.christianitytoday.com/ct/2021/december/deradicalization-deconversion-extremism-studies-test-middle.html.

Lord, act again. Lord, let us see it. Lord, remember compassion on us, he prays.

When you sit waiting for even more suffering to come your way, you can pray this, but still doubt that it is effective. Does God even hear? Is he the God who can rescue and wants to? Sometimes we're like the teen who feels no one is trustworthy, and even as we ask, we're not sure God even cares.

Habakkuk grasps our anxious doubt, and next the hymn reveals God's manifest presence, answering our plaguing questions of "Is he strong enough? And does he care?"

The Almighty God—He Is Able

As a college student, I was staying at a medical clinic in Texas, trying to figure out some of my strange health issues when a couple of the doctors came up with a new idea. They told me one afternoon that I may have a disease that would give me just a few more years of life. They said it with a tad more excitement than was warranted, I think because they were pleased to have an idea explaining my bizarre tests and problems. The illness would produce a host of symptoms, the scariest of which to me was losing my mental clarity (though some would argue that my ability to walk was probably dearer to me than I realized). I was in patient housing when I remember messaging with a friend and describing what I had heard that day. My verbal-processing brain was spewing words to get my mind around it, and yet I was facing God, asking him if he would be strong enough if this were true. Would he be there for me if this disease was real?

How strong is God? Is he strong enough?

Want to know how the hymn answers the questions? By looking at how God shows up.

In Bible literature terms, we call this a *theophany*—a description of a vision of God or sometimes an appearance. We find theophanies like this in a few songs of the Old Testament. They're wild, revealing power that is beyond our understanding. The imagery leads us in switchbacks up a mountain of startling descriptions. Even as we take in the powerful images, it can make us shy away from the astounding omnipotence.

Pay attention to the way the portrayal of God makes us feel his ability.

> **God comes from Teman,**
> **the Holy One from Mount Paran.**
>
> *Selah*
>
> **His splendor covers the heavens,**
> **and the earth is full of his praise.**
> **His brilliance is like light;**
> **rays are flashing from his hand.**
> **This is where his power is hidden.**
> **Plague goes before him,**
> **and pestilence follows in his steps.**
> **He stands and shakes the earth;**
> **he looks and startles the nations.**

> The age-old mountains break apart;
> the ancient hills sink down.
> His pathways are ancient.
> I see the tents of Cushan in distress;
> the tent curtains of the land of Midian
>   tremble.
> (Hab. 3:3–7)

God is coming, Habakkuk writes. That alone stops us in our tracks. He's engaged. He hasn't forgotten about us and this broken world. He comes. But his coming isn't an aimless wandering, and it doesn't say that he's coming toward us, as if we are the focus. Instead, the prophet wants us to see the route God is taking.

God is described as coming from the south of Judah. The Holy One is following the road his people took after he saved them from slavery in Egypt. As if he's saying, "Remember what I have done and what I am able to do?" "Selah," the psalm says, a phrase intended for pause, urging us to meditate on what was just said—*God is taking the exodus road.*

He's coming in power, like he did then. Have you ever been in a lightning storm and your curiosity turned to fear? To understand the strength of his glorious presence, the poetry puts us standing in the center of a storm. Flash! His splendor covers the sky, and rays flash from his hand. The brilliance and explosive thrust of lightning give just a taste of God's ability. It is reminiscent of when God met Moses on Mount Sinai in shining glory (Deut. 33:2), remember? Habakkuk's people would have remembered. He made a covenant with them that provided for them a law of life, and the infinite God wed his people.

In case we're still wondering about his ability, illness and war flank him. He used them for judgment on Egypt when he rescued his people. What's more, the Lord appears standing ready to act now, and even the earth and mountains obey him (Hab. 3:6). The earthquake reminds us of God's judgment and his glory, as he's shaken the earth in power before.[3] Those around us who would see his presence—they'd tremble at the sight (v. 7).

When we question the ability of God to act, this is where we turn—to what he is like when his active presence shows up. The people of Judah knew it; they could remember. The only way to express God's immense strength was with a vision that would petrify us or put us in awe that such a powerful God is for us and not against us.

If I rewrote Habakkuk's psalm from my experience, it would list the places God has revealed his power in my life. The hymn would say he was standing on the side of Highway 99W in Oregon. It was on that road that I prayed and asked the Lord to rescue me from my sin through Jesus Christ. Following my short car-prayer, it's hard to explain the powerful change I felt inside of me. If it wasn't so wonderful, I'd describe it as terrifying. I *knew* I wasn't the same; God himself had come to dwell

---

3. Andrew Wilson, *God of All Things: Rediscovering the Sacred in an Everyday World*, Illustrated edition (Grand Rapids: Zondervan, 2021), 16–17.

with me, though my language for it was fumbled at the time. Next the song would describe God walking from the green grass beside the highway down to the university in town where he taught me that the gospel wasn't just an idea to make my life easier, but essential hope for everyone. I would have been reminded of his powerful acts to rescue me from the ultimate consequences of my own self-sufficiency and pride.

The Lord met me that night in the Texan medical housing as I pondered if my life would ever be the same in light of the suggested diagnosis. While I didn't have a psalm about it, he reminded me of his power and salvation that made me his—he is able to care for me. It is the same truth Habakkuk sings here. Still, I'll tell you what you've probably already guessed—in the morning the doctors said something like: "Oh never mind. You don't have that condition now; maybe later." (I promise you, I really do like doctors still.) That night stayed with me. It meant that God was strong enough, even if I was on the journey toward death sooner or later, for we all are.

If it were you, what exodus road would God be coming from to remind you of when he showed you his power in past seasons? What road would assure you he was strong enough to rescue?

The question of God's power has been answered; his strength has been proven time and again, in the history of the Bible and, likely, the history of our own lives. Is God able? Can he help? Behold the Lord, who walks in with jaw-dropping power, and the response is obvious. *Yes.* Yes he is, and yes he can. Yet, while watching the powerful vision of God's appearance shows his infinite dominance, it still hasn't answered our other question. Is God willing to help us? Will he show up for our good? Is he the One who will take us where we need to go? The next lines of the psalm take us deeper into the purposes of the preeminent God.

The Almighty God Who Rescues—He Is Willing

You know in the boat when Christ's disciples have been terrified of the storm? They watch Jesus calm the squall with a word, and their fear doesn't leave. It just swings from targeting the raging waves to the One who just commanded the storm's obedience before their eyes. I picture their faces as they stare at Jesus, feet still wet from docking the boat and hearts still beating just as fast.

Habakkuk's listeners have been on a journey like that, once terrified by injustice and invasion, and now terrified by the power of the Lord. What do we believe about him if he is this strong?

The words of our hymn shift from describing the Lord in the third person to speaking to him in the second. This "conversation" with God is going to reveal his purpose, what he does with all of that alarming power.

> **Are you angry at the rivers, LORD?**
> **Is your wrath against the rivers?**
> **Or is your fury against the sea**
> **when you ride on your horses,**
> **your victorious chariot?**
> **(Hab. 3:8)**

What are you angry at, Lord? The Lord is clearly a mighty warrior, coming in battle, with fury, a chariot, and weapons, the next verses describe. *Are you angry at the rivers and sea?*

Habakkuk's asking about God's motivation. *What are you doing this for, God? Are you the type of God who helps?*

The bodies of water imagery paints a picture that God has rage coming against his enemies,[4] but that's not the entirety of his purpose. We get a taste of it with the description of his chariot; it's literally a "chariot of salvation." *That's* the kind of Almighty Divine Warrior he is. He is the Lord who will use "arrows" for *his* people (3:9). We're grateful for this detail, of course. And yet we still feel like the question regarding God's purpose hasn't fully been answered.

The hymn continues like an action movie, watching the warrior God walk through the world.

> **You took the sheath from your bow;**
> **the arrows are ready to be used with**
> **an oath.**
>
> *Selah*
>
> **You split the earth with rivers.**
> **The mountains see you and shudder;**
> **a downpour of water sweeps by.**

---

4. Bodies of water are often metaphors for the evil of the world and God's conquering of chaos as he opposes them. This passage brings to mind several rivers and seas God has "fought," the Red Sea, the Jordan River, the river Kishon. Ultimately, God will pour out his wrath on the "sea" and "rivers" (Rev. 16:3–4).

> The deep roars with its voice
> and lifts its waves high.
> Sun and moon stand still in their lofty
>   residence,
> at the flash of your flying arrows,
> at the brightness of your shining spear.
> You march across the earth with
>   indignation;
> you trample down the nations in wrath.
> (Hab. 3:9–12)

Even creation knows God's power, just as the disciples saw in the person of Jesus. In the presence of God, mountains writhe as if in labor. The deep floods sweep up, like in the days of Noah (v. 10). The sun and moon pause, entranced at the sight of God's glory and might (v. 11). Yet he has not come to ultimately move creation. No, his march is like a king in battle to deal with wicked nations, like he has done in the past and will do again (v. 12). The justice God foretold against the Babylonians will come, and it will come by his hand. *Remember what I've told you I will do,* God implies.

Our thoughts return to the questions in verse 8 and we think: *Answer the questions, God. Where is your fury going and why? Why would you come ready to fight?*

If God is one who says he will show up, and I'm supposed to trust that he will, I want to know his strength isn't purely bent toward destruction of the wicked. I want to know if he uses his power for more—if he is willing and wanting to help his people. As we wait in the exhausting suffering that is the injustice of our world, how do we know he is? Has he forgotten us? Does he rule over this chaos for a reason completely opposed to care for you and me?

Finally, the answer comes.

> **You come out to save your people,**
> **to save your anointed.**
> **You crush the leader of the house of**
> **the wicked**
> **and strip him from foot to neck.** *Selah*
> **(Hab. 3:13)**

God comes to save his people.

Let this sink in. This is God's purpose for using his power—he rescues his children from their enemies. He shows up to deliver.

His gracious care is coupled with divine judgment, for he's also going to crush the leader of the wicked. The prophet helps us recall the defeat of Pharoah, the coming defeat of the Babylonians, and even the defeat of the evil one whose head was promised to be crushed by the son of Eve (Gen. 3:15).[5] They are going down, for our God wins.

So we see that the answer to our first question ends up being the same for our second. "Is our Lord willing to help us?" Yes. Yes, he is. When circumstances appear

---

5. The Hebrew in this verse for "leader" is literally "head" as in Genesis 3:15. You can read more about the connection to Genesis 3:15 in James M. Hamilton, *God's Glory in Salvation through Judgment: A Biblical Theology* (Wheaton, IL: Crossway, 2010), 253.

to be the worst conceivable, we can pray: "God, revive your work! And let us see you do it!" like Habakkuk did (v. 2). We can sing his hymn and know God is powerfully able and devotedly purposed to care for us. He not only administers justice to his enemies, he rescues his people.

As I get older, I have to write more and more things down: voice memos on my phone, notes on half a dozen pads of paper strewn across my house, software to organize my screenshots, and *everything* on a calendar. I don't just glance at my calendar once a week. I don't just read my to-do list on Tuesdays. I review them all the time. Because I need lots of help to remember. God and Habakkuk know we need help to remember too, especially as we wait. When we pray in a broken world, we can remember how the powerful God works for our rescue. He's set up reminders for us.

Remembering to Look to the Future

God works in patterns.

I told you I grew up on rural land in Oregon. My parents raised horses across the street from acres of state-owned cattle and forest land. When we began training a young horse on a lead, we'd begin with patterns. We wanted him to be able to predict what we'd do next, so we worked the same way each day. Putting on the halter, over his nose and ears, leading him a handful of steps across the paddock, turning to the right, and walking back to the stable to stop a few feet early for a treat—out, around, and through the mulch to return.

The mischievous colt came up with every excuse not to pay attention. He'd sniff an overturned bucket, as if he didn't know what it was, then attempt to jump into my arms when the cat leapt onto the nearby fencepost as a spectator. You can imagine how that doesn't work with a five-hundred-pound lap-dog-wanna-be. Eventually, after a lot of training, he'd follow the sequence—out, around, and through.

The repetition guided him through the sequence of how we would work, so he knew me and my cues.

God knows we're not much smarter than a yearling sometimes. We desperately need all the help we can get in remembering who he is and how he works. Graciously, he works in patterns too. He does the same thing over and over, showing his character, his purposes, and his care for his people. By describing the Lord doing the works of rescue in the past, it reassures us of God's power to crush the wicked and points us to the work of rescue he will do again.

We remember for the future.

If we keep reading, the hymn further describes God's conquering of his enemies, asserting God will turn his enemies' power against themselves, as their weapons reverse (v. 14). He will do it years later with the slanderers of Daniel who had him thrown into the lions' den only to find themselves with the lions after their plan failed. God will do it again many years later with Haman who wanted to hang Queen Esther's cousin Mordecai and ended up hung on his own gallows. And one day

the Babylonians who came to scatter Habakkuk and his
neighbors would face the same powerful God.

> **You pierced with his own arrows the**
> > **heads of his warriors,**
> **who came like a whirlwind to scatter**
> > **me,**
> **rejoicing as if to devour the poor in**
> > **secret.**
> **You trampled the sea with your horses,**
> **the surging of mighty waters.**
> **(Hab. 3:14–15 ESV)**

The very next verse reminds us of how God used
the waves as horses to crush the Egyptians who chased
the seemingly helpless Israelites out into the wilderness.
The Lord opened the Red Sea for them to walk across
on dry land and then used the water at his command to
rescue his people and conquer the others.

The imagery consistently hints back to the time
of the Exodus when they were enslaved and in need
of God's salvation. Do you see the words being used?
God reminds them of his mighty acts of plagues, his
conquering their enemies, his glorious presence with
Moses, his quaking of the mountain (Mount Sinai) when
he came down, and his leading them up to the land.
Why does he point them back there over and again? The
Exodus is the heart of their salvation. It's the pattern he
set, as a gracious God who was going to work in power
and kindness to an undeserving people. He rescued and
called them into relationship with himself, providing for

them every step of the way. *The Exodus is the pattern of the rescue that the people of Habakkuk's day leaned into, but they knew a second exodus was coming.*

Beginning with Moses, the people heard they would need another great work of God, this time including within their hearts. God would gather his people, freeing them and providing a spiritual rescue (Deut. 30:3-5; Jer. 16:14-15, 21). For in Habakkuk's day, the prophets had already been prophesying about the new exodus that would center on a new Moses, a new deliverer, but he would be from the house of David (Amos 9:11-12; Micah 5:2-5).[6]

Look again at Habakkuk 3:13: "You come out to save your people, to save your anointed." God is going to save his people and the one he has chosen—the anointed one. To call someone "anointed" means he is marked, as if with holy oil on a priest or king. The kings in David's family are often called anointed ones and pointed to one Anointed Servant who would deliver and reign with justice—the Messiah.

So when Habakkuk explains the Lord's motivations for working in the world, he says the Lord will save the anointed one, a king in the Davidic line in the time of Habakkuk. But he's also going to save the Anointed One. It would be better translated: "through whom he will save."[7] The Lord is going to rescue his people, and he's

---

6. For more on this, see L. Michael Morales, L. *Exodus Old and New : A Biblical Theology of Redemption* (Downers Grove, IL: InterVarsity Press, 2020).

7. An interpretation is that the term means "with," and is presenting God's "anointed" as having a different relation to

going to do it through his Messiah. God will save powerfully through the second exodus.

Habakkuk is remembering to throw us into the future.
We remember the exodus pattern of rescue, for the God
of Sinai was still working. He's the God who continues
his pattern of rescue, rescue from the shackles in Egypt
through the Red Sea, rescue from the bondage of sin
and death through the life, death, and resurrection of his
Anointed One. Ultimately, he will rescue from the injustice
and evil of this world. We sing along with Habakkuk so
that we remember God's patterns. His consistent steps to
take us out, around, and through to the goodness he has
for us in a New Creation defined by his rescue.

We remember when we are trembling and questioning
God. We remember when the cancer treatment doesn't
work. We remember when the adoption falls through. We
remember when we're praying for peace instead of war
for our brothers and sisters in Christ on the front lines.

We remember the patterns of the past that tell us of
the future rescue, even if we remain now in the chaos.

Once I was swimming in the Adriatic Sea, off the
coast of Croatia, alone in the water with my roommates
sitting on the rocky beach we'd found. I'd figured out
that if I dove to the bottom, about fifteen feet down, I
could find all kinds of things, including sea cucumbers.
I dove down again and had just reached out to gently

---

salvation from that of the *people*. God's salvation is for his people,
but it is accomplished with his anointed. O. Palmer Robertson,
The Books of Nahum, Habakkuk, and Zephaniah, 2nd edition (Grand
Rapids: Eerdmans, 1990), 237.

touch another slimy tube-like animal, when I heard a bang. The sea began to spin, which is just as disorienting as it sounds. Feeling flipped and dazed, I'm grateful I remembered what my scuba instructor had said many years ago—the bubbles. I blew out and swam after the air bubbles to the surface. I was dizzy and confused as I floated to the shore. It wouldn't be until days later that I would learn I had blown my eardrum, sending my equilibrium into a spiral. I didn't remember from my scuba instructor that the first fifteen feet have the greatest pressure change when you're underwater, and I needed to diligently clear my ears. But I did remember the pattern of the bubbles. Bubbles always go up.

Habakkuk calls us to remember what is always true—the pattern. Bubbles always go up and the powerful Lord of the covenant rescues his own. We sing it even when the world spins. We remember that our God is able and willing to save. That's exactly what he's done in the past, and he will do again one day to make all things right.

Do It Again

We learn the patterns of the world and live accordingly. Or we should anyway. Once I was talking with a handful of college students at our church. They sheepishly admitted that a van-full of them had decided to drive a couple hours to the beach in the middle of the night to watch the sun rise over the ocean. Friend, we live on the *West* Coast. The sun has never risen over the Pacific Ocean when you're standing on an Oregon beach, and it never will, though it has some pretty great sunsets. I laughed and tried not to laugh too hard. Their exhausted brains fumbled the decision late at night while celebrating having finished finals. They ignored the patterns we know happen each day; the sun rises in the east.

Our God who acts on behalf of his people is more able than we can imagine and more willing to rescue us than we dare hope. *He is the God who rescues his people.* It's the pattern, not of the world, but of its Maker.

Habakkuk is reminding the people of the gospel they had—the gospel pattern from the exodus rescue.[8] So we sing Habakkuk's psalm and remember the power of God in his salvation through the second exodus. When Jesus Christ was baptized, he came up out of the water and saw the heavens torn open. The Spirit of God descended on him, and a voice from heaven said, "You are my beloved Son; with you I am well-pleased" (Mark 1:9–11). Marked as the Son, Jesus was the representative of the true Israel, out in the desert (Exod. 4:22; Ps. 2:7) and the Anointed Servant in whom God delighted (Isa. 42:1, 3). The trinitarian God had brought the new exodus. God had come down in power to redeem his people again.[9] God was powerfully present, working to rescue.

---

8. Timothy Keller, "Rejoicing in Tribulation" (Sermon Series: Living by Faith in Troubled Times, Redeemer City Church, n.d.).

9. Richard Bauckham, *Who Is God? (Acadia Studies in Bible and Theology): Key Moments of Biblical Revelation* (Grand Rapids: Baker Academic, 2020), 94.

His pattern is the testimony of God's faithfulness to us, as we wait for him to do it again. We know he will bring all things to justice, but we still pray, "Lord, rescue today."

I've read the book of Acts and seen broken, Spirit-filled people work toward unity and obedience and God's miraculous power to save and bring justice.

But in the last year, I've heard of dear friends manipulated by pastoral leaders. I've seen churches divide over self-promotion and self-protection rather than care for the hurting among them. I've seen denial of prejudice when it is obvious to all observers. I've stared at this psalm of Habakkuk and needed his words to prompt me to say, "I've heard what you've done before, my God. I stand in awe of your grace, righteousness, and love, that we see in the work of Jesus. I remember what you did to make yourself known in the book of Acts. I remember your work among your people. *Do it again and may we know it.* In judgment, remember compassion."

Maybe you're like me, and you've needed the reminder, when you want to believe that God is able and willing to work. You've needed a script for the response of faith, even when God has not yet answered your prayers. Habakkuk gives that to us.

So we pray or sing: "Do it again, Lord. You've worked before. Do it again."

Chapter 8

Faith with Utter Loss

"God, I will wait and trust."

*"That whenever signs of God's wrath meet us in outward
things, this remedy remains to us—to consider what God is
to us inwardly; for the inward joy, which faith brings to us,
can overcome all fears, terrors, sorrows and anxieties."*

John Calvin, French theologian, reformer,
and pastor in the sixteenth century[1]

H er smile could light up a room. She would sit and
laugh with me in our church foyer, talking about
the silly mix-up she'd had that week, and you wouldn't
know that other stories my Middle Eastern friend could
tell would give you nightmares. The murder of her father
by the local Islamic leaders, the fleeing for their lives, the
grief and fear involved in coming to America. Yet this
woman had more genuine joy than those who haven't
faced a teaspoon of her suffering.

---

1. John Calvin and John Owen, *Commentaries on the Twelve Minor
Prophets*, vol. 4 (Bellingham, WA: Logos Bible Software, 2010), 175.

It's perplexing. The waiting she'd dealt with while terror chased behind makes us think there's no way she could go on. Fear of that nature often paralyzes and leads to hopelessness. The loss can sprout bitterness, and any concept of joy is buried like the dead. In this uncertain world, you too have faced fear and loss, so what is the path to joy through the pain?

Our lamenting prophet has walked her same road. He's felt his share of anguish. After his grief-stricken lament, he heard the way of life is the way of faith, so he's written a hymn for his scared and brokenhearted people. He's giving them words for the impending loss.

The lyrics prayed for God to revive his work again, like the first course in a plated dinner set before Habakkuk's people. The hymn progressed to a dazzling and fearsome feast of God's presence and work. He's the Almighty Divine Warrior who saves his people, displayed with pictures of rescuing chariots and lightning flashing from his hands. He is both willing and able to rescue. And his plan to save through his Anointed One has not been forgotten.

The psalm then turns immensely personal; this is where we pick it up. The rest of the song expresses the individual response to the horror Habakkuk knows is coming—the Babylonian conquerors. They're coming as a consequence of the people's disobedience, long foretold in the covenant. Habakkuk exudes fear, grief, and—surprisingly—joy.

Habakkuk isn't normally labeled the prophet of joy, but I'd argue with anyone who says otherwise. He doesn't do the "fake smile" that makes your face hurt. He's not one of Job's friends, telling the people to accept the suffering as their own due. Instead, he models trembling faith in the waiting that allows him to sit in fear, grief, and joy at the same time. And he would teach us it's possible for us too.

Faith and Fear

Fear is a common part of our lives, as we all look to what will happen next. Like mini-prophets, we try to look into the future, and when we don't like what we imagine, we're scared. Like when your doctor tells you that her next test is going to "pinch a little," and you know what that means. Or, more seriously, when you hear the anger mounting and see the fists clenching in the person across from you, and you've been there before. Or when you see a car behind yours swerve out of the corner of your eye, and your heart races. You suspect what happens next is going to hurt.

Habakkuk looked ahead and knew things were going to get worse. Signaling a new section of the song, the prophet uses the word with which he began the hymn. In the beginning, he prayed to the Lord that he "heard the report about you," and now he sings of having heard what will happen to Judah . . . and is afraid. Sometimes fear is a response of faith. In this case, it was.

The Lord would bring the prophesied consequence of exile through Babylon. Their lives would never be the same. Habakkuk knows woes will come against the wicked invaders (Hab. 2:6–20), and he's just reported a vision of the Lord coming in power and judgment to save (3:3–15). The alarming power of God and the gravity of the situation aren't lost on him.

His reception to the news turns physical, with four lines building on the description of his visceral reaction. Have you ever heard something and felt the response in your stomach? That's a taste of what our prophet is describing.

Here's what he says:

> I heard, and I trembled within;
> my lips quivered at the sound.
> Rottenness entered my bones;
> I trembled where I stood.
> (Hab. 3:16a–b)

He sings that he's been trembling, literally in his gut (you can imagine the repercussions of that), and his lips quivered. He cried to the point of sobbing and shaking.

I told a couple friends about this verse as we discussed some of the life-shattering decisions before them. After a silent pause, one said, "Isn't it beautiful that that's in the Bible? It describes real life." "Yeah, it's like having a panic attack," the other said with a look that could relate.

Fear can have all kinds of impact on us. In the last year, your lips may have quivered and stomach cramped, afraid. Maybe you've wanted to run. God stands ready to hear, like the parent who wants to hear about the child's nighttime fear rather than telling her to "pull yourself together." David did this in the Psalms. "Fear and trembling grip me; horror has overwhelmed me. I said, 'If only I had wings like a dove! I would fly away and find rest'" (Ps. 55:5–6). The Lord hears from desperate David and meets him.

Waiting, Habakkuk tells God they're trembling! Then, he has the people sing their faith. Here's the rest of verse 16:

> **Now I must quietly wait for the day of distress**
> **to come against the people invading us.**
> **(Hab. 3:16c)**

Habakkuk is afraid, yet here's the hope: he believes what God said. Even in his fear, even in panic, he believes God will do what he promised, which means he knows his powerful God will ultimately bring justice on the bloodthirsty and greedy coming their way. He leads his people to believe that God will take care of his people and deal with the wicked. They're waiting for God to work because they trust him.

Isn't this where we sit so often when we're afraid? Waiting for God to do something. We know what he's said, and we have to decide if we're going to wait in faith or just in terror. What if his promises of justice, even if not met in our day, sustain? Faith in waiting means remembering. Habakkuk had just sung of the vision of the Lord's coming as a warrior riding in to rescue his people. His power is enough to shake the world and crush his enemies (vv. 6, 13).

So, we remember God literally shook the world when the divine Son died and when he rose from the grave (Matt. 27:51; 28:2). He told his people, "Do not be afraid. I have overcome the world." He crushed his enemies in his victory of the cross. And when his Spirit-filled, newly born church preached the gospel and faced threats by the religious leaders, they prayed for boldness and more miraculous works to point to Jesus. Then God shook the place again and answered their prayers (Acts 4:23–31). One day he will come as the Divine Warrior to judge evil and rescue his people again, with an earthquake as never before (Rev. 16:18). This is the God we remember, even if we are the ones shaking for now.

We trust in God's power to act, and we also revere him for it. It's as if the fear of circumstances and the unknown morphs into a holy fear of the Lord, a trusting awe that, while we tremble, produces hope from deep within us and washes into peace. For the term "quietly wait" (Hab. 3:16) implies something more than stubborn anticipation, but a stillness of soul, a rest. We may fear, but our fear of the powerful God assures us that he will handle the evil we face.

The stubborn belief that God will handle evil is what I remember from the witness of early Christians. My husband, mother, and I toured the catacombs in Rome, when we spent a few days exploring the city. The ancient tunnel systems spread several kilometers in labyrinths. Outside the city, the tunnels were used from the second to the fifth century, primarily by Christians who didn't have a safe place to bury their dead. Deep underground, individual slots were dug out in the walls for the bodies of believers and sealed with clay. Paintings and carvings surrounded the dead. The time-worn art expressed the faith of our ancient brothers and sisters. As we walked together in the dimly lit tunnel, the guide told us of the persecution that put many into the burial walls where we stood. She pointed to the symbols you could still see carved with intention and interpreted them for us. She spoke as an academic who had given the lecture hundreds of times, but as she got to the imagery of the earliest saints, their faith could be anything but boring. They were very likely to have been martyred, killed for their faithfulness, and a couple symbols repeated on their tombs. They simply meant "I have peace" and "I will rise again."

The faith of the dying and the faith of their church who buried them had something to say to those who could kill the body but never harm the soul—*I will rise again. You cannot keep me down. I may die, but I am not over.* They knew that God would take care of his people, and he would handle the injustices they faced.

Habakkuk wasn't going to see God's judgment of Babylon; he was going to die in exile, just like those under persecution in Rome. Still, he believed God would ultimately bring his people back from captivity, another rescue, caring for them like a mother for her children. The promise of the Messiah, the Anointed One, would still come from this people. And God would judge those who caused them harm.

Like Habakkuk and our early-century spiritual siblings, we make powerless those who would harm us by remembering and trusting that God will keep his promises.

Fear can take us the other way, not toward trust in a God who works for us, but toward our own way. When was the last time you saw injustice and only wanted to flee? Fear gets the better of us, taking control while we ignore what we've been taught. It's like the time as a child I walked the gravel road a mile to my friend's house, only to encounter a mountain lion standing under the bridge in the woods. I'd been instructed dozens of times not to run if I met a cougar, but my body didn't let me have a choice in the matter. Run I did. Thankfully, the large cat returned to her drink in the creek, uninterested in the kid scrambling up the hill.

Church, while we may be afraid, at times we as a people have frantically fled from the sight of trouble instead of believing our God. Just as frenzied, our fear may rise, and we respond with anger, even lashing out. We accuse those around us and alienate and villainize to deal with our uncertainty. Friend, we've seen these very responses only multiply in our divided times, especially within the church. Have you been on social media?

Other times, our fear paralyzes us, like an artic wind freezing us in place, and we hide, refusing to deal with the news given. Brother or sister, we've done this too instead of dealing with scary situations. It's then that denial attempts to create its own version of the truth.

Habakkuk points us to remember the powerful, fearsome God, opposed to a response of fight, fright, or freeze that looks only to ourselves. God's people sing when things will get worse before they get better; we know he is the God worthy of our life of faith—and faithfulness.

Faith and Loss

Have you ever had a repeated injury and the doctor continues to restrict your activity? What began as a small deal kept getting worse and the reinjured limb now needs even more protection than before. You're restricted to the point that life feels impossible; you just keep losing. Or perhaps the stress presses from another angle. At first, you're keeping all the budgets balanced, but then water begins dripping from the ceiling. The repair costs are wild. The next day, your car "bumps" that obnoxious pillar in the parking garage, and the bill from a recent emergency doctor visit arrives in the mail. The finances are hemorrhaging, and you're about to hit empty. It feels like loss, loss, loss.

Whether it's been an injury, a bank account, family, or a community, you've likely had a time when the losses compounded. Maybe you've even wondered how you'd survive. The list of things taken away feels longer than what is left.

That's the picture Habakkuk paints next. After admitting his fear and his decision to wait with trust, he sings of the suspected hardship approaching—utter loss that compounded exponentially. He describes destruction of the nation and follows it with some of the most moving verses of faith in the Bible.

> **Though the fig tree does not bud**
> **and there is no fruit on the vines,**
> **though the olive crop fails**
> **and the fields produce no food,**
> **though the flocks disappear from the**
> > **pen**
> **and there are no herds in the stalls,**
> **yet I will celebrate in the LORD;**
> **I will rejoice in the God of my salvation!**
> **(Hab. 3:17–18)**

If an invading army is coming, then he knows nothing they have will remain. Disaster is coming on the land—a total economic collapse.

This poetry describes the loss of agriculture that would have sustained and given stability. Beginning with what would be less devastating, the prophet walks the people through each line of infertility. First, he sings that the fruit and figs don't grow. Okay, this means the source of sugar has dried up; hard, but not deadly. Next the olives fail. No oil for skin, medicine, worship, cooking, or maybe burning. Next, no grain from the fields which means no bread, no storage for winter. Then if the flocks die out, they will gain no wool and no lambs. Finally, the stalls are empty, leading to the shortage of meat and milk. There will be no help to work the ground and move wood. The poetry is describing famine conditions. In our

FAITH WITH UTTER LOSS

days, it would say "though there be no grocery store, no Amazon, no electricity, no clothing, and no blankets."

The background of this list is a covenant where God had promised to provide for his people. Do you remember the covenant blessings that Moses promised them, along with the curses (Deut. 28)? God is removing his provision of fruitful farming that he wanted for them in the Promised Land. The sin of many had consequences on them all. As every last line of human hope slips through their fingers, sending them adrift in poverty, Habakkuk has something to say.

He will still trust the Lord, his covenant God. He'll celebrate him in loss—before deliverance.

His statement is shockingly tender and resolute. The description of the collapse hits us like a ton of bricks. If we lose all of our financial and societal stability, would we still walk in faith? I've experienced unfair loss, though never at the level of this catastrophe. Yet my loss felt devastating. I'm betting you have walked that road as well. The in-between time of waiting for rescue as the reliable slips through your fingers. So how do we walk in faith in utter loss?

Habakkuk would say it is by declaring our God is better than anything we could ever lose. The Giver is better than any of the gifts. The relationship with God was not all about his material blessings. It was about the true God who loved and saved them and would continue to be faithful to them.

So even in the loss of the good gifts of God, Habakkuk says his faith will stay. It's the vision of Habakkuk 2:4

lived out. God's people choose faith because they know that it is *by faith in God* they will live. The righteous shall live by faith.

Habakkuk lands us where the Scriptures do over and over again, at God's feet, recognizing the great value of knowing him over everything else. Habakkuk looked toward the coming devastation by the Babylonians, and Jeremiah looked back on their destruction of Jerusalem. In his lament, Jeremiah comes to the same conclusion. After describing gut-wrenching suffering, he counters it with the worth of knowing God and his great trustworthiness.

> I say, "The LORD is my portion,
> therefore I will put my hope in him."
> The LORD is good to those who wait for
>   him,
> to the person who seeks him.
> It is good to wait quietly
> for salvation from the LORD.
> (Lam. 3:24–26)

At times, do we become overly focused on our blessings from God, so much so that we are beside ourselves when they are gone? The blessings may even be good things, as Habakkuk lists, but they are not ultimate. What if the entitlement of our culture seeps into us and the loss that slips down the drain is leading us to contempt and control instead of tenderness and trust? It's as if the prophet takes the "what if that happens" from our lives and turns it into "yes, even if that happens" as an act of hope.

He knows the good gifts ultimately won't come from the work of our hands but from the hand of the Lord. The details we know, but Habakkuk didn't, is that God's generosity will mean one day building materials will be as lovely as the most expensive jewels and metals (Rev. 21:18). The beauty we see in a lake and a sunset will be surrounding us as we worship the God we most deeply long for. The wrongdoing we face today will be judged, and we will stand in the judgment not condemned, because of the life-giving death and resurrection of Jesus Christ. It is on that day when we will see most clearly that living by faith was the way in, around, and through to the best destination.

Habakkuk sees the loss of God's blessings and the economic collapse in their not-so-distant future. Even as he does, the prophet is not negating any trauma received. Grief and pain may also remain. Still, he knew though God's gifts may be lost, God's faithfulness wouldn't be.

If we are stripped of everything, what then? Still faith, Habakkuk says. Faith and joy.

Faith and Joy

Who celebrates during a pandemic? I'll tell you that our family had a "party" weekly, for the sake of survival. It's not nearly as impressive as it sounds; it wasn't an intentional act of defiant joy. No, rather parenting a two-year-old in an isolating pandemic meant her creativity ran wild, along with her desire to interact with anyone other than her parents, and our willpower was often drained. When she declared it was another stuffed animal's birthday, who were we to keep her from setting up the entire house with balloons, birthday hats, noisemakers, streamers, and (pretend) cake? "Party house" took on new meaning.

In reality, when do we celebrate most? Not most of us during a global pandemic. It's when the things we've been longing for finally come. When goals are met after years of work—a promotion or a graduation is cause for a gathering. Bring the family, friends, and feasts on out. When it's time to rest, eat, and give gifts on holidays, we know how to have a good time. It's normal to celebrate when God's good gifts surround us.

But, rejoicing in the bleakest of times is peculiar. We might look at someone with a cancer diagnosis smiling and think: "They just don't get it yet." Or we watch someone who's been out of work for too long, whose family's pile of bills is looking like a cell phone tower, still filled with contagious happiness. One might think he's not understanding the situation. With loss, we expect not only grief, but to be accompanied by discouragement and pessimism.

That's not how Habakkuk saw it. Uniquely in the writings of the twelve Minor Prophets, we find Habakkuk setting the example for choosing joy in disaster. It's not that he ignores the loss or grief, but that joy and

heartbreak coexist. His sorrow can drive him into celebrating what he will always have in God.

Read these soul-stirring verses again and imagine
God's faithful people at the temple collectively singing
the lines after hearing Habakkuk announce what was
coming.

> Though the fig tree does not bud
> and there is no fruit on the vines,
> though the olive crop fails
> and the fields produce no food,
> though the flocks disappear from the
>   pen
> and there are no herds in the stalls,
> yet I will celebrate in the Lord;
> I will rejoice in the God of my salvation!
> (Hab. 3:17–18)

In the draining of all food sources, with an empty
fridge, Habakkuk said he would rejoice in the God he
knew. Grief can push us into bitterness, with broken
expectations and pride. Or it can humble us, throwing us
toward the One who is still the Lord, the God who makes
and keeps us. Loss can make you angry, and indeed, God
can handle our angry lament. Yet it can also make you
more tender and grateful.

Habakkuk guides the people to promise how they
will react. His words are striking. He pledges his joy with
the strongest expression. In the Hebrew, it's as if he
says, "May I celebrate!" "Let me rejoice in God!" urging

himself on in delighting. He emphasizes his will—his choice of response.[2]

Does it sound unreasonable to expect such joy out of someone? Do you feel it's too much to ask of you? With no deliverance yet in sight, Habakkuk speaks of taking joy in God. How can we do this without acting like a child "cleaning" his room, the one who just shoves the undesirable trappings into the closet? This isn't a "shove your feelings" commitment of the prophet.

Instead, he's doing what he's done through this entire song. He can praise because he has remembered. Recall where this song began? He asked God to work again. Then he records the frightful vision of God's power and mighty deeds of salvation, for he is the God who rescues his people. The memory of God's past deliverance allows him to praise with joy even on the darkest days.

Habakkuk's invitation is not to manufacture joy like what you'd have on a tropical beach (#blessed). It's not the kind of joy that a pushy friend demands as he wants you to "move on," pressuring for a moratorium on discussing trouble. It's the kind of gritty joy you find in a hospital room, in a counseling office, and sometimes through tears in the middle of the night. It's joy that trusts while it waits, even if sorrow intermingles.

---

2. It's not unlike what Peter told the Christians scattered across the world of the early church. They had chosen to rejoice, even though they "suffer[ed] grief in various trials," because they knew what their faith would bring—the salvation of their souls. So they rejoiced with "inexpressible and glorious joy" (1 Pet. 1:3–9).

And so for you, friend, I extend some questions. Has the Lord delivered you from the domain of darkness (Col. 1:13)? Has his love been better than life (Ps. 63:3)? Has his goodness enveloped you on a warm day when the sun's rays touched your skin? Has his Spirit taught your heart to say "Abba, Father" because you are his (Gal. 4:6)? Then, brother or sister, when the losses pile, we will still celebrate.

I'll tell you, I understand why Habakkuk put this in a song. He knew people sometimes needed to sing. Sometimes I need to sing.

One Sunday several years ago, I arrived at church with what felt like a broken heart. Another scandal about a leader in ministry came to light, but this one I knew personally. I felt betrayed, confused, and angry. My husband would have told you that I had spent the previous couple of days quietly stewing and, out of the blue, bursting into tirades about ethics, accountability, humility, and the evil of a seared conscience. Yet there I stood in church, and I sang. Not because I felt like it, but the faith of those around me supported my weight in the community of voices. As I sang, tears flowed. The sorrow didn't leave, but the words that spoke of the work of God refreshed my memory of his faithfulness. So, while the grief remained, I could also say because of my church on that dark day, "I will take joy in my God."

In this uncertain world, friend, sing with me. For, faith triumphs through the choice of joy. It is how a hymn begins with a desperate prayer of "I have heard

the report about you . . . revive your work" and turns
into a victory song (Hab. 3:2).

The Pioneer of Our Faith

You and I have had to wait before. Maybe we've
waited with fear for news about a desperately needed
apartment after the landlord had made a wisecrack
about if we'd "fit in the neighborhood." We've waited
after news that we were going to lose things precious
to us: health and ability to work as we have in the past.
We've waited with fear and grief.

Jesus, the Son of God, who lived the human life in
its fullest—he waited too. The Lord Jesus saw what was
on the horizon—his suffering and death. He knew it was
the plan of God, the plan of the Father and the Son from
long ago. He responded to fear physically with sweat like
drops of blood. He knew the agonies before him—loss
before deliverance would come. He stood where we
have been. Yet he looked to the joy that was better than
what he would endure. He knew the promises of God to
be true, just like Habakkuk did.

The author of Hebrews puts it like this:

> Let us run with endurance the race that
> lies before us, keeping our eyes on Jesus,
> the pioneer and perfecter of our faith. For
> the joy that lay before him, he endured
> the cross, despising the shame, and sat

down at the right hand of the throne of
God. (Heb. 12:1b–2)

He is the pioneer and perfector of our faith, it says.
That means he's the foundation and the One who will
bring it to completion. He models living by faith in the
trustworthiness of God, and he proves to us how trustworthy God is. For by him, deliverance from our sin
has come, and our future deliverance is certain. In the
meantime, in the waiting, his goodness is still the best
thing we could taste.

Normally we protect the things we value for fear of
loss. We put them in safe deposit boxes. We insure them
and remodel them. We put padding around our children. Still, the thing of greatest worth in our lives needs
no theft deterrent. The riches of knowing God through
Christ, we can never lose.

The Joyful Wait

That friend I told you about at the beginning of
the chapter? As a young woman growing up on the
other side of the world, she'd had a dream. A dream
about truth from a book—a book she knew to be a New
Testament though she'd never seen one. After finding
a New Testament, she knew. She needed the truth that
was Jesus. Her life was turned upside down by a Galilean
man who had lived, died, and rose again for her. Her joy
stood on something much greater than the dangers her

faith posed or the anguish caused by the radical politics of her community. So she sings with Habakkuk.

No armies are marching toward my city as I write, but we, too, fight our fears with knowledge of the steadfast and fearsome God. We can look at coming loss and cling to the most valuable in Christ rather than the most desirable that could slip away. We give up the spiraling worry that can steal hours of our lives as we consider the "what-ifs" of loss. The life of faith beckons with invitations to joy, even in the sorrow—for the Lord is trustworthy in the turmoil.

Conclusion

God: *"I am your salvation and strength."*

"But I will look to the Lord;
I will wait for the God of my salvation.
My God will hear me."

(Micah 7:7)

As the news of the COVID-19 virus filtered into Lesotho, a small country encompassed by South Africa, some Christians braced themselves. How would they endure this? Early on, some believers thought God had miraculously spared the vulnerable community, as no cases were reported, though it was clear that testing wasn't being done properly yet. For others, the dread of what was coming made them seriously consider if their communities would survive.

You see, the medical system was already taxed under normal circumstances. Living in rural areas, people were often three to eight hours by foot from a town where they would find a medical center with nurses that worked faithfully to deliver babies, wrap wounds, and provide consistent medication for the 23 percent of the country that was HIV positive. There wasn't a lot of confidence in the ability of these centers to cope.

Most houses lacked running water, and people walked daily twenty to thirty minutes to find some. How would they do handwashing? Several of the comorbidities were common problems for people in the region, and doctors didn't seem to know what the virus would do to the neighbors with HIV. In a country of 2.5 million people, they had one ICU that couldn't handle even one critical COVID case.

When the cases came, the border with South Africa shut down—the entire border, as it's an island within the larger country. With lowered commerce and the inability for ordinary people to travel, supplies lowered. My friend in the capitol looks back and remembers when she realized she would go without real coffee, but she also remembers the fears of needing to isolate from the rural children's center she directs where sixty-five children live. The seventeen local staff who lived on-site admirably took on their education as schools closed. Then, things got more serious. People went hungry. Misinformation ran loose. Tests took weeks. Fears loomed that if you got sick, there wasn't any help. The fear wasn't unfounded.

God's people in Lesotho sought the Lord. They needed what they couldn't provide themselves.

Habakkuk knew this yearning. He felt the dread of devastation on the horizon. We get to the very end of his book and now, to the very end of his hymn. Habakkuk knows he cannot provide for himself. Instead, he gives

us a response to his entire conversation about brokenness and suffering. He writes lyrics about who God is in
the chaos of this world.

The Hymn's Voyage

Remember when you heard an answer to your
prayer, but it was *not* the answer you wanted? You
prayed with faith only to receive a resounding "no"
when you were sure the answer would be yes? So it
was with Habakkuk and his people, who waited not for
God to correct the corrupt leaders of Judah, but instead
heard he would send the entire nation into captivity.
Someone has said that how you respond when you don't
get the answer you want is the true test of character. If
that's true, Habakkuk was training in spiritual formation
with his song. He taught how to respond when you don't
get what you want.

Habakkuk took his listeners on a voyage with the
psalm he wrote. At the helm, the prophet navigates
through the fog of disappointment. He begins with a
prayer—*I've heard about you, Lord! I'm in awe of your
deeds.* Then he eases the request to their mouths:

> **Revive your work in these years;**
> **make it known in these years.**
> **In your wrath remember mercy!**
> **(Hab. 3:2b)**

Next, the song comes into open waters with a vision
of the Lord God in all his power and glory. It has the

frightful feeling of a storm, revealing the inexplicable might and rule of the Lord through imagery of brilliance and lightning. The ship tosses in the journey. The vision of God is terrifying while also consoling with the memory of his work at the Exodus. He is the Warrior God who has saved his people from their enemies before and will do it again.

The violence of the storm turns into strong tailwinds ushering the people into reminders of who their God is. It blows the singers into the final section, where they respond in honesty. Fear and sorrow arise at the acknowledgment of what is coming—enemies who will trample them. Faith comes to their lips. They will wait in trembling faith for God to do what he said, to judge their enemies. With a list of conditions that describe a destitute poverty, they affirm their choice to take joy in the Lord. The boat floats to the tranquility of the destination, and the people sing:

> **Yet I will celebrate in the Lord;**
> **I will rejoice in the God of my salvation!**
> **The Lord my Lord is my strength;**
> **he makes my feet like those of a deer**
> **and enables me to walk on mountain**
> **heights!**
> **(Hab. 3:18–19)**

The hymn lands us in a cloistered marina of praise and declarations of faith while the winds of what's coming still beat on the reality of life. Who is God for his people and for us today? He is our salvation and our strength. Ultimately, he is the God who gives life, even when you don't get what you asked.

The God of My Salvation

When Habakkuk writes his vow to rejoice in God, he uses titles for God that hint at his source of joy. It shouldn't surprise us, for Habakkuk has used this name many times before. The Old Testament writers use the name of God, the Lord, Yahweh, as a reminder of the God who took his people out of slavery and made a covenant with them at Mount Sinai. The readers of the book would have seen those four Hebrew letters and knew exactly what that title meant. "Oh, he's the God who made us his and him ours." He's the One who defines faithfulness, compassion, and steadfast love—the true Creator God. In *this* God, Habakkuk says, we can take joy.

In the parallel line of the song, he calls him the "God of my salvation," which isn't far. For who is the Lord if he isn't a God who has saved them in the Exodus? The root of this word has been repeated through Habakkuk's hymn, so the singers would have felt it reverberate in their souls. He rides chariots of salvation (3:8). He comes out to save his people (3:13). He is the God of salvation (3:18).

Most of the time when someone loses everything that provided for a safe and stable life, they would call God "the God of my judgment" rather than "the God of my salvation." But that's not where Habakkuk goes. He recognizes that God's salvation is more than his physical provision, and he decides to celebrate him. It's something so astonishing it almost feels inappropriate in the heartbreak, like someone singing joyfully at a memorial service. Yet you and I have probably praised God at one of those services, because we know what Habakkuk does. He's not laughing at another's grief. He sees joy because of something much greater than death—our God who will keep his promises of salvation.

Even in the chaos of all that we need taken away, God is the One who stands as our salvation. He rescued us from the darkness and corruption we find inside, and one day he will finish the rescue from all of it in the world. His salvation isn't purely a freedom from a cruel master, like Pharaoh, though it is a freedom from sin and the devil. Rather, the salvation is tender and personal; he makes us his own children, pulling us into his family. We may lose, but we will never be deprived of God.

It was going to get harder, and though Habakkuk wasn't getting his prayers answered how he wanted, he was going to be cared for in how he needed. He had the God of his salvation.

God, My Strength

In certain circumstances I pride myself in being strong. I'm a superhero in the face of strong-as-steel blackberry brambles that overrun our Oregon yards each spring. I don't shrink back from the invasive vines that shred your skin if you're not careful. I've got it handled. But I could list the ways I'm weak. Like many did, I felt extremely weak when the news of COVID-19 began. I wasn't concerned for myself, but I couldn't stop the deaths of friends of friends, nor could I soothe the exhaustion of the medical workers. Though I'm not naturally given to anxiety, it was hard to keep all the balls in the air except with short, desperate breath-prayers while thinking about all the families in our area at home with kids and the needed incomes lost.

When else am I weak? My chronic health issues mean, on bad days, my functionality wanes. Let's be real, on those days, most of my effort goes into attempting kind interactions with those around me, because we need supernatural Spirit-filled help to exhibit kindness when in pain. On other days, I've panicked at relational conflict that felt tangled and unfair. Spirals of conversations have left me praying those desperate breath-prayers and wanting to hide in weakness. None of us are inherently strong enough for life, friend. We don't have what it takes in ourselves.

Habakkuk has come to realize this. Though he is weak, he knows where support comes from. The final verse of the book begins:

> **The LORD my Lord is my strength.**
> **(Hab. 3:19a)**

Habakkuk speaks about his Lord who is the God of the covenant—the Sovereign King who is also his master. This God strengthens me, Habakkuk says. He gives me his power, his courage, his stability, so that I can stand. I may be drained of all I have, but God is never depleted.

In immense suffering, the prophet knows his relationship with God isn't fleeting like the winds of good or bad fortune. He is consistent, no matter what, firm like God's covenant promises that do not change.

To close his psalm, Habakkuk repeated lines from David's Psalm 18. It was when the king of Israel said the Lord has made him strong.[1] The shepherd-boy-turned-ruler told the story of God's rescue in his life. He had seen the Lord guard, equip, and defend him. It was God who deserved the credit for his success and victory over his enemies. When David had been weak, the Lord had made him stand. Here's what Habakkuk echoed from the famous king:

> **The LORD my Lord is my strength;**
> **he makes my feet like those of a deer**
> **and enables me to walk on mountain**
> **heights!**
> **(Hab. 3:19)**

Habakkuk takes the words of David and applies them to himself. The strength God provides makes his people so steady they can walk up on the high crags of the mountains. Up there an enemy cannot grab them and cannot surprise them. Habakkuk isn't going to fight as a warrior, standing at the crest of a bluff, like David might, but he knew the God who made him strong.

---

1. Throughout Psalm 18, David attributes his protection, rule, and success to the hand of God. God's work defines his reign, so much that this song is also in the extra material of 2 Samuel 22.

The prophet recognized it would be dangerous up on mountain heights if he didn't have his feet under him. The cliffs are steep, and the rocks are loose. A drop could be deadly, but the mountain deer don't fall. God makes the treacherous-yet-advantageous places secure for his people. It's on the high places one can see what's coming without fear.

Friend, God gives us strength such that the scary can be safe, the things that we would expect to knock us down only reveal your stability. In the heights, with our feet supported beneath us, we can look to the future and trust in our God. In the heights, we can see what our God will do. Adversity was approaching, but Habakkuk knew he would have what he couldn't give himself—strength.

Strength when we cannot stand. Strength when we've lost it all. Strength when our hearts are angry or scared. Strength when we bear the injustice. Strength when we wrestle with God. The God of salvation doesn't save once to leave us alone, like a mama turtle laying her eggs in the sand and hoping for the best. No, he makes our feet to stand beneath us, even if we feel weak.

We may feel alone. We may walk through a dark night of the soul. But Habakkuk teaches us that honesty, humility, and dependence is the way of life, even with questions or fears (3:2, 16). God's provision for us is a stability in chaos and enabling power—strength—just like the believers in Lesotho had.

The adage "God doesn't give you more than you can handle" implies we each have some sort of self-created ability to overcome, and God, like a good waiter, doesn't fill our cups over that line. This is far from biblical. Instead, in the suffering, God is present. He is Sovereign King, the Strength-Giver who holds our feet stable.

For Habakkuk, God is the limitless Lord. But this powerful God is also near and intimate as the God who offers strength. In Habakkuk's book, God is the One who always has the power.

Power and Providence

Power. Everyone wants it. From the social media fight for influence, to the mudslinging in political campaigns, to the small child who says, "I'm the boss!" We often don't have as much power as we crave.

This book has been a discussion of power of sorts. Those with power chose violence and selfish gain, both the powerful in Judah and the Babylonian army. And God has the power to judge both, in his time. Yet with his same power he will uphold his own faith-filled remnant.

Ultimately, power isn't owned by the rulers of nations, as God proves. Neither is power fully ours. Power belongs to him. God owns it all. When our strength is drained, runs dry, depleted, God reigns sovereign. The powerful Sovereign Lord is the salvation of his people and their daily strength.

In the end, Habakkuk accepts God's providence, even as his people will be taken into exile. He anticipates loss, yet believes that the ruling God will keep him alive in the suffering. In the chaotic world, our recognition of his power means we can tremble at what's to come and still believe he will make us stand firm on the heights.

Habakkuk's Journey and Ours

Habakkuk has been on a journey in this book. Do you remember his angry prayer at God for not showing up? He's modeled us how to pay attention to the pain around us, and to turn that into lament. He's also questioned and wrestled with God's actions, reminding us our God can take it. Oh, but the Lord didn't leave him without hope. He told him the way to survive: the righteous live by faith. This would be the central line Habakkuk would work to live out.

God called Habakkuk to live by a faithful faith, but that wasn't to blow off his own responsibility toward justice. God's woe song revealed his plan. The Lord spoke of oppression and what he would do. It's comfort for the hurting, and it's conviction for us who have messed around with power over others. (That's probably all of us, wouldn't you say?) He will judge, and he's bringing his glory to fill this earth, every nook and cranny. We've seen it come at the cross and resurrection of Jesus, and it's spreading now.

So we come to the final chapter, Habakkuk's hymn of waiting and joy . . . and faith. The prophet wonders internally: "What does faith look like in this chaos?!" Then he takes a breath and writes a psalm to sing to ground the roots of faith in our hearts. He asks God to do what he's always done and to have compassion—mercy. He sings of his power and purposes. He sings of fear, loss, and joy. He sings with trust in the God of our salvation and our strength.

Habakkuk diaries his journey from a lament to trust, through pain and questions. We can picture him trembling in anger, in fear, in desperation, and in awe. It was God's grace working in him, for how else do we explain the endurance, understanding, and transformation we read in this book? This is good news, because God's grace is working in us as well.

Your life of trembling faith in this chaotic world will likely mean living some days in lament. It's living with your eyes open, even when it hurts to look at the brokenness and injustice around us. It's choosing to wrestle with God and speak to him instead of just about him as you hide. It's walking beside those who lament and those who question. Friend, it's leaning into God's grace as he shapes us in the heartbreak of seeing the broken world.

The life of faith is the courage to face injustice with Spirit-empowered kindness and patience for God's work. It's seeing the misuse of power for how God sees it and repentance when we've been complicit. It's evangelism that acknowledges the pain of the abused, the God who sees injustice, and the Savior who took the cross for them. It's reading a woe song about corrupt oppression and responding with advocacy for the dignity of image-bearers, while looking toward the day when God's glory will replace the wicked.

The life of faith is singing with God's people a prayer for God to revive his work, even when dread and catastrophe are on the horizon. It's believing that he's the God who has saved us in power and will save us to glory. He has conquered his enemies before, and he will finish the job.

Our faith holds joy in suffering, for we will never lose God. He is our daily source of strength and stability.

The Life of Faith in Chaos

God's Word doesn't only inform us; God's Spirit uses it to change us. The book of the prophet Habakkuk is the Word of God, and we are different people by reading it.

So lament like you see injustice for what it is. Pray like God will hear you, even if you're afraid, outraged, sad, or distressed. Believe that the Lord who worked in the past is still the God who will judge the oppressors and save his people. And sing with determined joyful trust in the God of your salvation and your strength, for he is better than all the things we could lose.

You've walked with Habakkuk up the hill and seen from the heights what God says he will do, his promises of justice and call to faith. Now go with that panorama in mind. Believe him and live.

Sister or brother, may the Lord comfort you in your laments. May he meet you in your wrestling. May he give you courage to see. In his righteousness, may you be reminded of his justice. By his power, may you see him